The Designer's Color Box

A Guidebook and 75 Cards for Creative Combinations and Inspirational Ideas

Sean Adams

Abrams, New York

Introduction

DESIGN IS 90 PERCENT PERSUASION. We don't convince a client to choose an option simply because it is "cool," but because it is the best solution to their problem. Alternatively, color is subjective: one likes what one likes. Color is emotional, not rational.

Years ago, a client asked me for a specific shade of green: Jaguar British Racing Green. I extensively researched Jaguar automobile paint colors from 1922 and found multiple color charts including British Racing Green. Yet the client rejected every version I presented to him with the same green. He insisted that the color on the project was not British Racing Green, even though I had documented evidence. This green existed only in his imagination, rooted in the memory of his grandmother's green Jaguar from decades before. Then I understood. I asked him to look at the color outside and, voilà, it was indeed the correct green.

The light in which we view color influences how we see it, and the names of colors affect our feelings toward them. For instance, "moss" sounds much more appealing than "slime." This deck of cards offers seventy-five color names that, hopefully, evoke positive associations. Additionally, lighting conditions play a crucial role in how colors appear. You can test this by moving the cards to different environments or, as I often do, by taping them to a wall and viewing them from a distance over time.

Finally, here is a useful tip: no color dislikes another. There is no wrong combination, regardless of the plethora of rules. If you like a palette of colors, apply it with confidence. The only poor color combination is one approached tentatively. Color gives us a voice.

The Cards

WARM COLORS 1–22

1. Butter
2. Lemon
3. Yellow
4. Mustard
5. Tangerine
6. Orange
7. Burnt Orange
8. Peach
9. Coral
10. Navajo Red
11. Warm Red
12. Red
13. Scarlet
14. Salmon
15. Carnation
16. Pink
17. Magenta
18. Violet
19. Lavender
20. Periwinkle
21. Lilac
22. Purple

COOL COLORS 23–42

23. Royal Blue
24. Midnight Blue
25. Navy
26. Blue
27. Cardinal Blue
28. Sky Blue
29. Ice Blue
30. Seafoam
31. Mint
32. Turquoise
33. Peacock Green
34. Teal
35. British Racing Green
36. Forest
37. Emerald Green
38. Green
39. Kelly Green
40. Tea Green
41. Lime Green
42. Chartreuse

EARTH COLORS 43–57

43. Avocado
44. Pistachio
45. Eucalyptus
46. Olive Green
47. Khaki Green
48. Moss
49. Sage Green
50. Tan
51. Coffee
52. Brown
53. Burnt Umber
54. Chocolate
55. Chestnut
56. Harvest Gold
57. Ocher

NEUTRAL AND SPECIAL COLORS 58–75

58. Wheat
59. Beige
60. Sandstone
61. Greige
62. Putty
63. Pewter
64. Slate
65. Charcoal
66. Gray
67. Light Gray
68. Parchment
69. Sand
70. Cream
71. White
72. Black
73. Fluorescent Pink
74. Gold
75. Silver

Butter

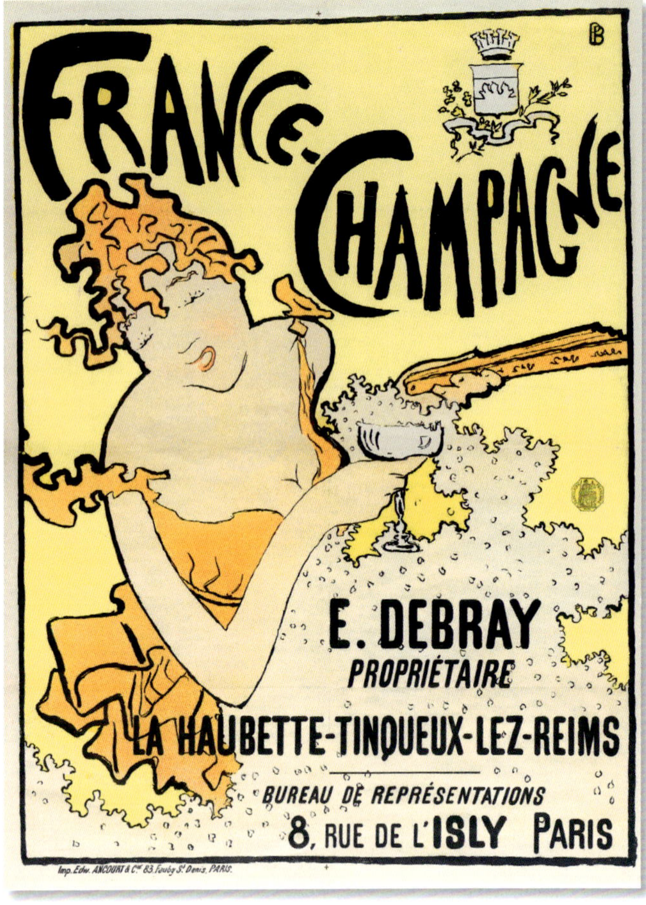

1

France-Champagne

Pierre Bonnard ~ 1891

POSTER

Japanese prints and artists such as Henri de Toulouse-Lautrec and Jules Chéret influenced French artist Pierre Bonnard. He applied large areas of flat color to his poster designs to create a sense of space, while allowing the viewer to add the details. This design's bold expanses of butter and yellow, simple forms, and high-contrast typography addressed the need for advertising in complex urban environments such as Paris.

Lemon

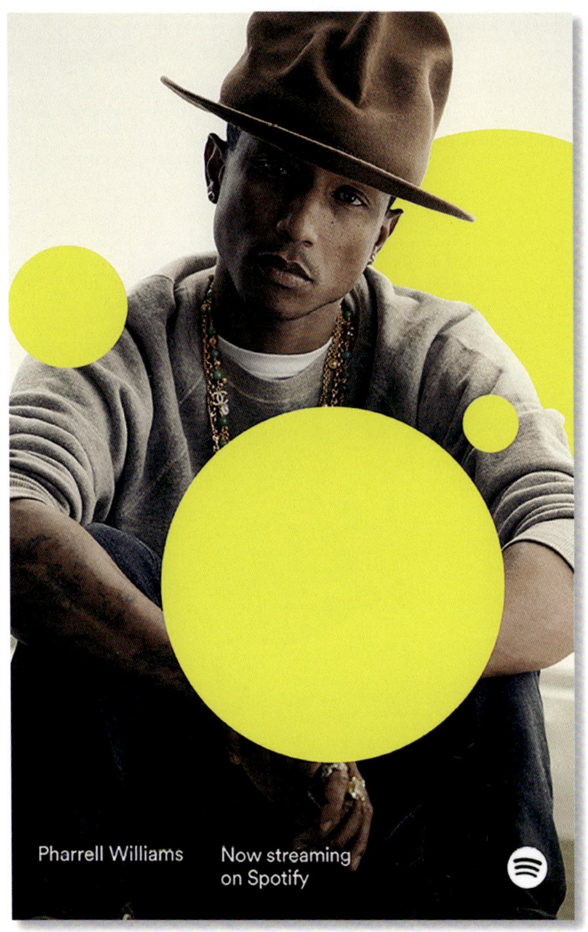

2

Pharrell Williams, Spotify

Collins ~ 2020

BRANDING

Collins' rebrand for the streaming music service, Spotify, is inspired by the visceral reaction that occurs when an individual makes a personal connection with a song. Music makes listeners cry, cheer, scream, sing, or dance. The intense colors—such as this ultrabright lemon—and graphic forms capture that moment with a visual system that serves to reflect the soul of the Spotify brand.

WARM COLORS

Yellow

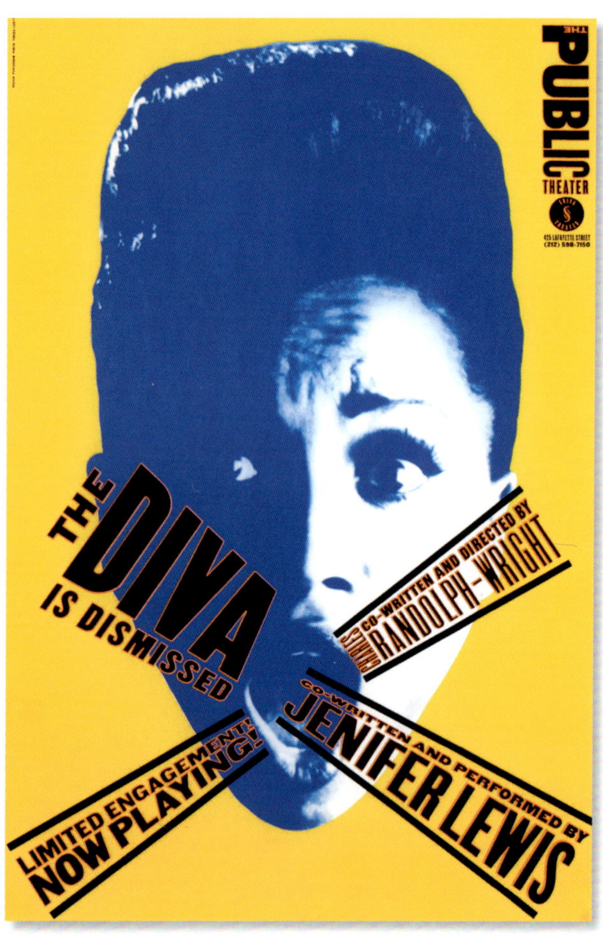

3

The Diva is Dismissed

Paula Scher ~ 1994

POSTER

In 1994, graphic designer Paula Scher redefined the theatrical poster using bold typography and intense colors. In this example, for New York's Public Theater, she merged hip-hop, New Wave, street typography, and Russian Constructivism into a new visual language of extreme energy. The vibrant yellow, blue, and black poster jumped from the walls in the gray, urban New York environment.

WARM COLORS

Mustard

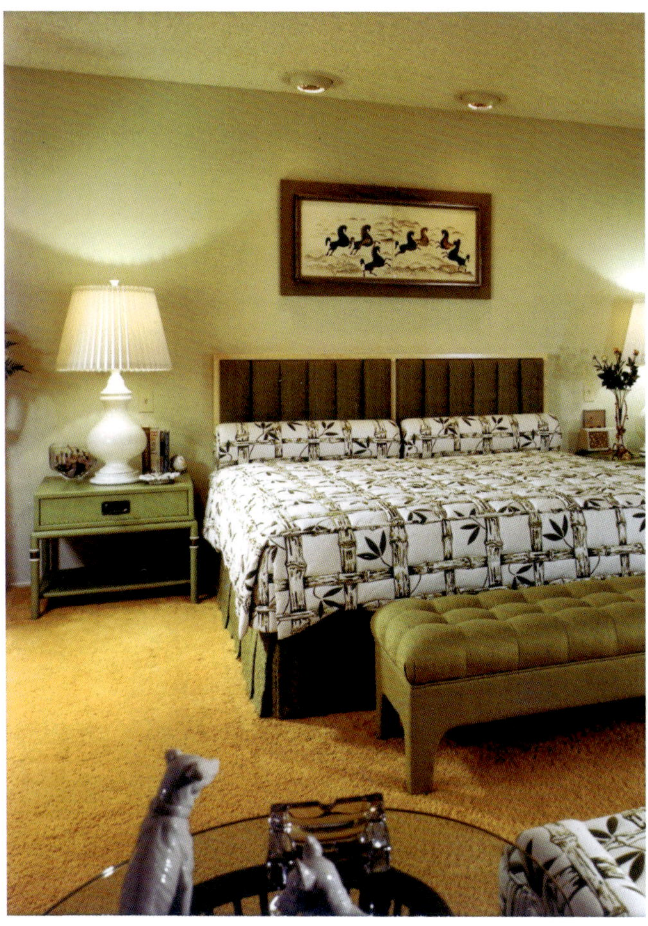

4

Canyon Estate Interior

George Szanik (photographer) ~ 1969–76

INTERIOR

The colors we associate with the late 1960s and early 1970s—mustard, avocado, harvest gold, and ocher—were a response to the counterculture and environmental movement of the 1960s. The materials may have been synthetic polyester, but the veneer of a natural color made the consumer believe they were "at one with the earth."

WARM COLORS

Tangerine

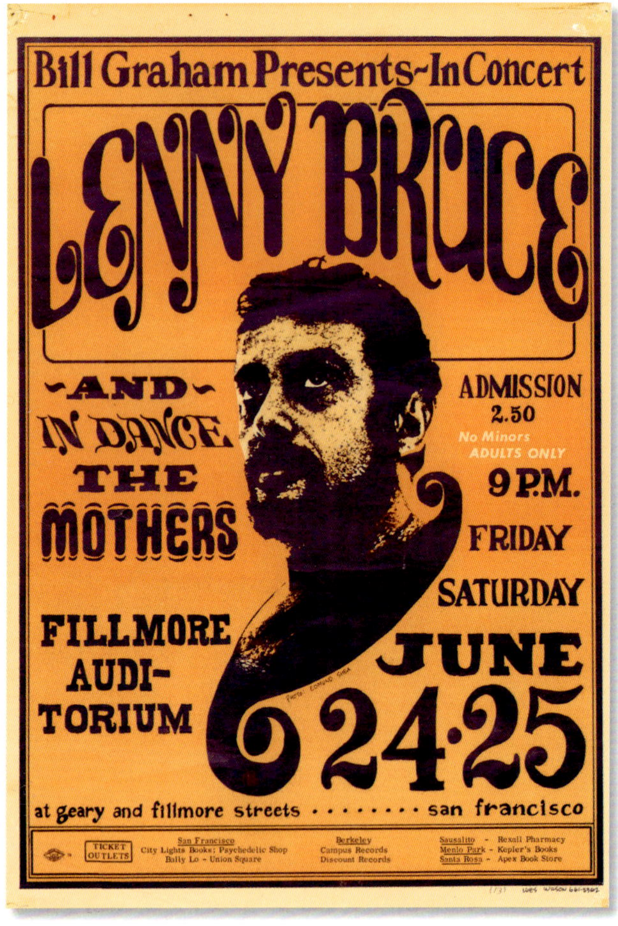

5

Lenny Bruce

Wes Wilson ~ 1966

BROADSIDE

On this broadside for Lenny Bruce, artist Wes Wilson worked with two colors, low-budget printing, and hand-drawn typography to promote an event at the Fillmore Auditorium in San Francisco. Like other examples of the Fillmore poster movement, the flat color references nineteenth-century posters such as those of Pierre Bonnard. Unlike Bonnard, Wilson mixed colors unconventionally, here tangerine and purple.

Orange

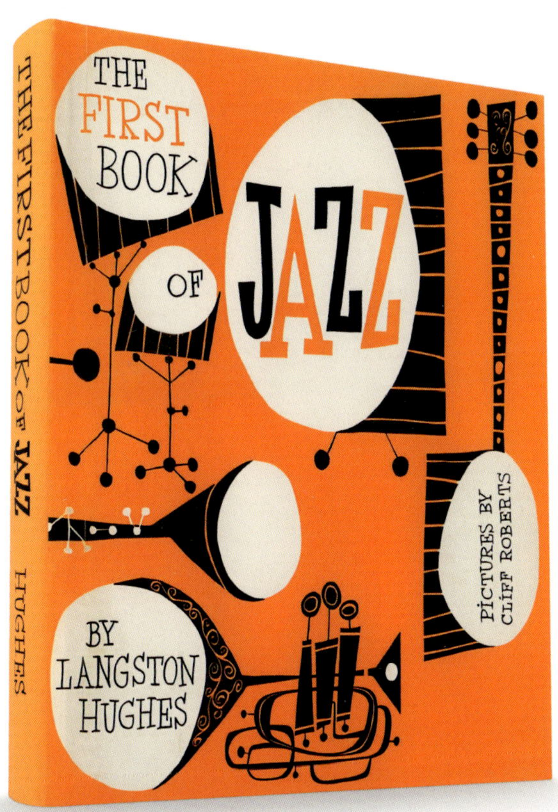

6

The First Book of Jazz
Cliff Roberts ~ 1955
CHILDREN'S BOOK

Part of the *First Book of...* series, this volume by Langston Hughes follows the career of Louis Armstrong and the growth of jazz in the twentieth century. Cliff Roberts illustrated the book with a bebop and spontaneous flavor to echo the jazz content. The color palette of orange, black, and parchment white are wonderfully aligned with sophisticated urbanity rather than a more conventional children's book palette of primary colors.

WARM COLORS

Burnt Orange

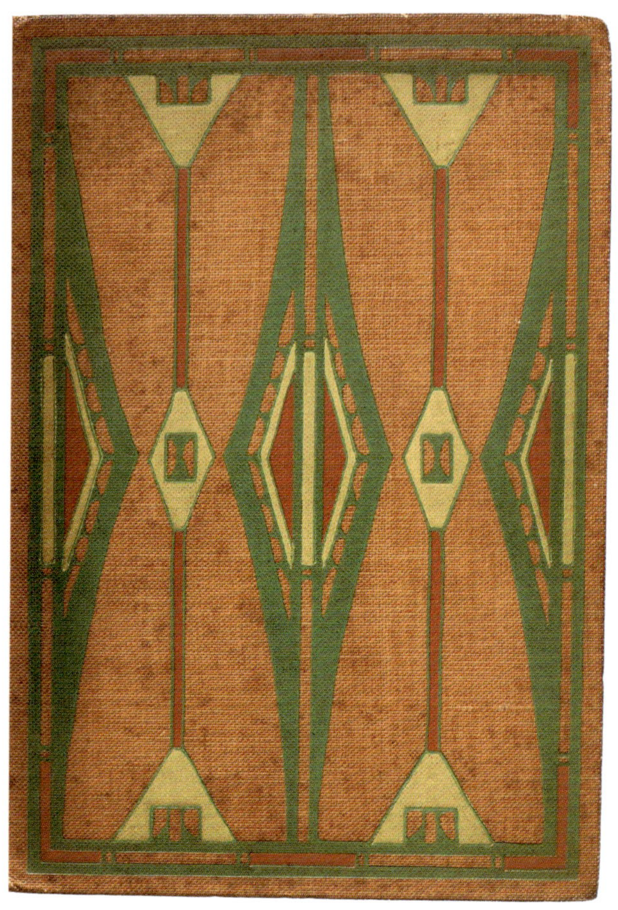

7

The Indians' Book

Henook-Makhewe-Kelenaka (Angel De Cora) ~ 1907

BOOK COVER

Author Natalie Curtis Burlin and designer Angel De Cora created a book to preserve Native American songs at a time when it was illegal to perform them in public schools. De Cora incorporated Native American pattern and iconography with colors from plant-based inks. Burnt orange is associated with creativity in many Native American tribal cultures.

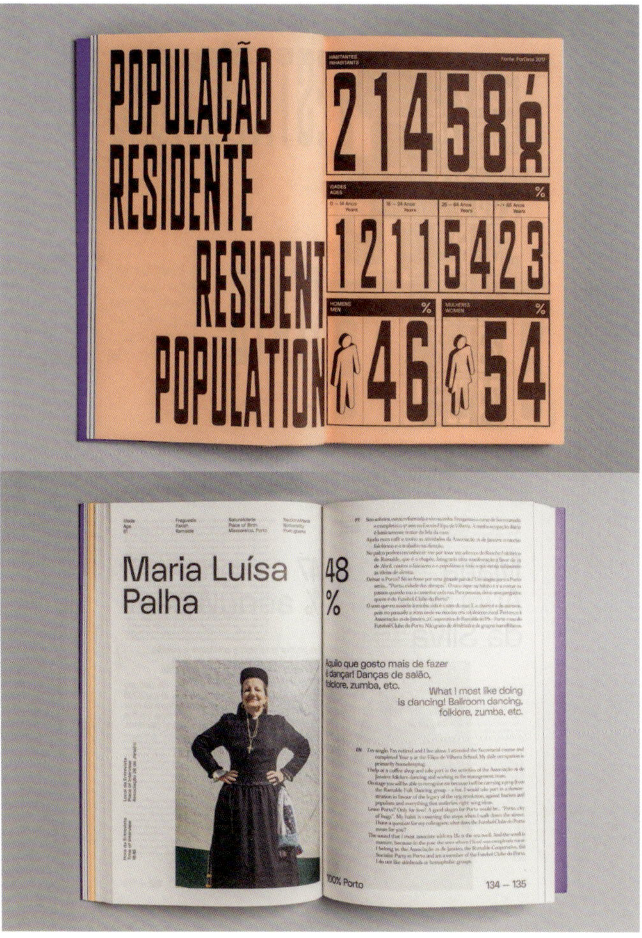

8

Teatro Municipal do Porto

Oscar Maia ~ 2019

PUBLICATION

The Portuguese city of Porto is known for its exquisite colors and diverse culture. For a publication celebrating the city theater's eighty-seventh anniversary and Rimini Protokoll's production, *100% Porto*, graphic designer Oscar Maia worked with peach, purple, vernacular typography, and the stories of one hundred inhabitants of the city. The combination is a publication that is distinct to the city, its people, and its unique flavor.

Coral

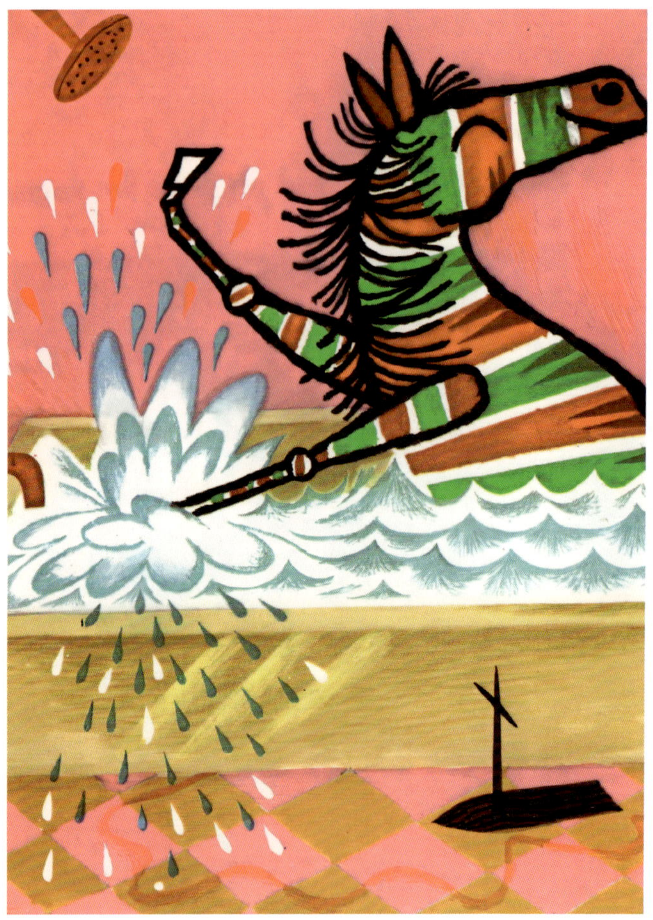

9

Alexander by Harold Littledale

Tom Vroman ~ 1964

CHILDREN'S BOOK

Harold Littledale's most loved book follows the activities of a boy's mischievous, imaginary horse. Alexander splashes in the bath and jumps on the bed. Of course, the true culprit is the boy. Tom Vroman's genius was to illustrate Alexander as a multicolored zebra in a Technicolor world. Vroman's use of unexpected color extends beyond the green and red zebra. The coral bathroom tile paired with an ocher bathtub is sublime.

WARM COLORS

Navajo Red

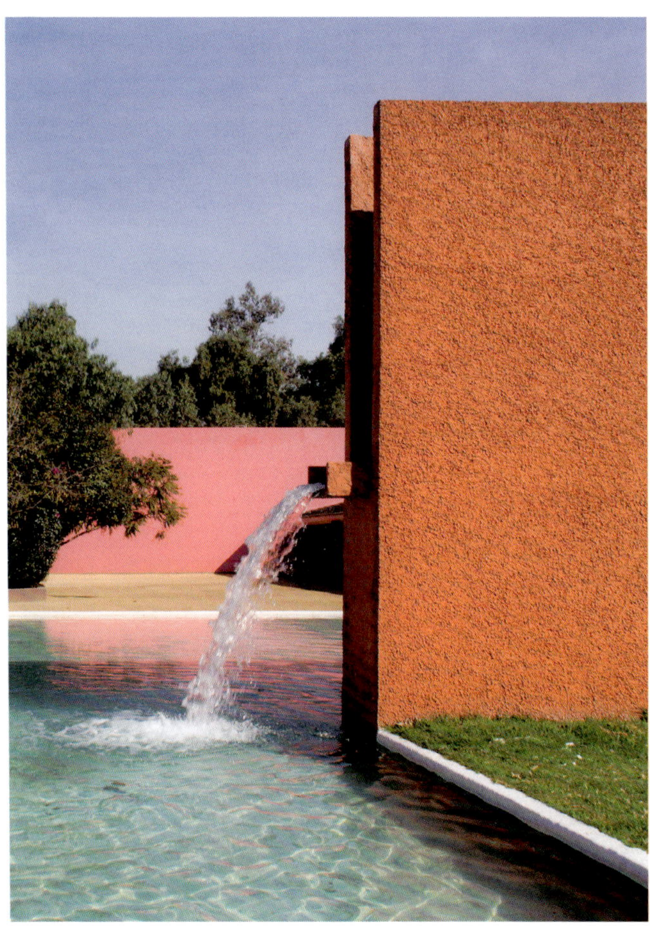

10

Cuadra San Cristóbal, Mexico

Luis Barragán ~ 1966–68

ARCHITECTURE

Architect Luis Barragán said: "Any work of architecture that does not express serenity is a mistake." His design of the complex Cuadra San Cristóbal responds to Mexico's physical geology with multiple planes and minimal geometric lines. He incorporates traditional colors such as Navajo Red, and adds Moorish themes of surface, water, and light with pink and blue to create a feeling of serenity.

WARM COLORS

Warm Red

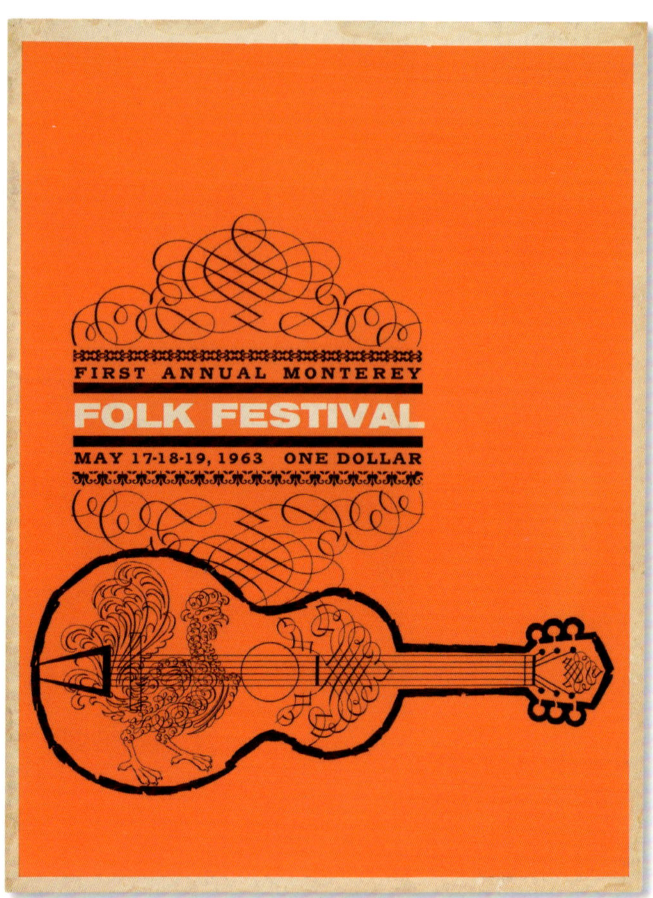

11

First Annual Monterey Folk Festival

Unknown ~ 1963

EVENT PROGRAM

The Monterey International Folk Festival was a three-day music festival in Monterey, California. The event saw early appearances by Bob Dylan, Joan Baez, Jerry Garcia, and Janis Joplin. The program's cover embodied the theme of counterculture California with a bright, warm red echoing the state's sunsets and poppies.

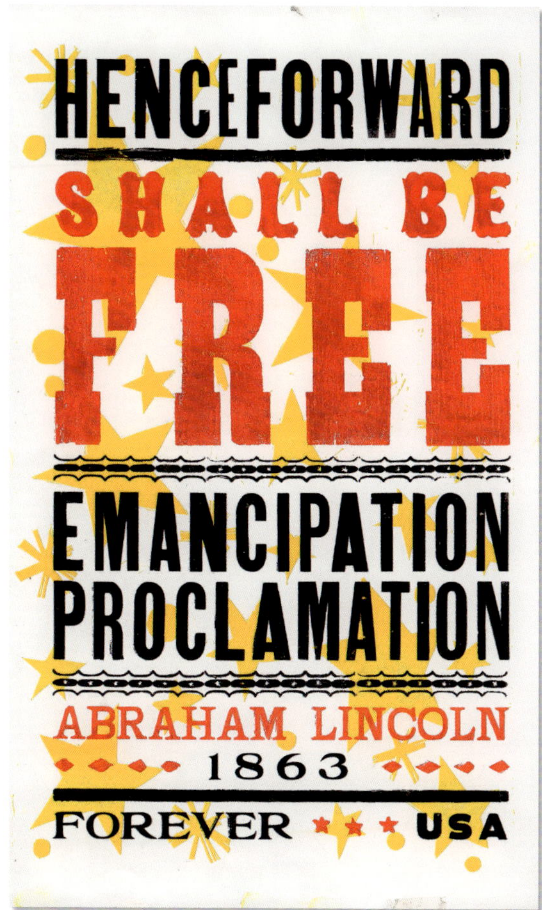

12

Emancipation Proclamation

Gail Anderson, Antonio Alcalá, Jim Sherraden ~ 2013

POSTAGE STAMP

The team of Gail Anderson, Antonio Alcalá, and Jim Sherraden of Nashville's Hatch Show Print produced this commemorative stamp for the 150th anniversary of the signing of the Emancipation Proclamation. To reference the nineteenth-century, they worked with letterpress typography, and used red, yellow, and black for high-dynamic contrast, and to remain true to nineteenth-century production methods.

WARM COLORS

Scarlet

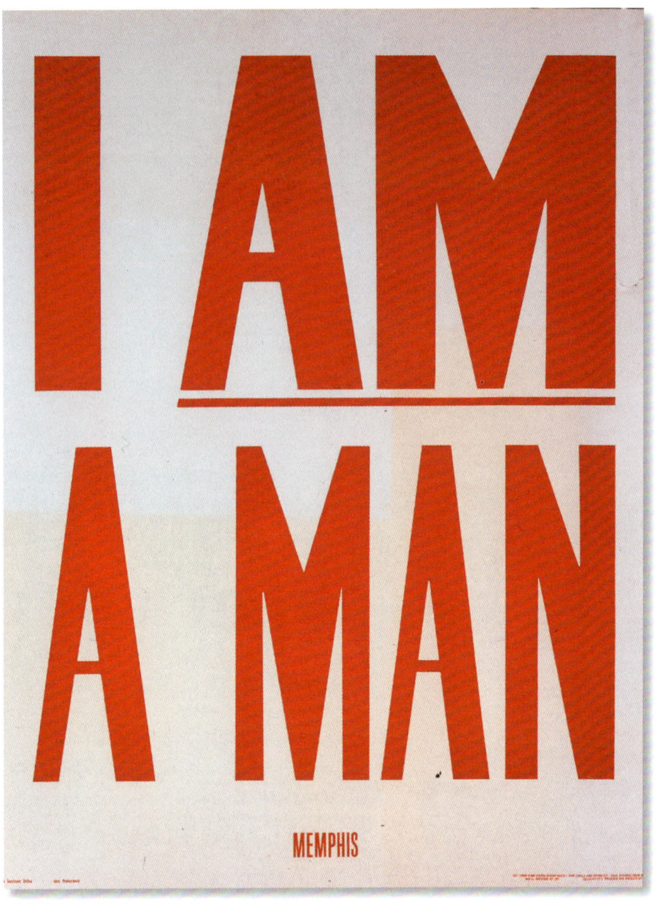

13

I Am a Man

Emerson Graphics, Tea Lautrec Litho ~ 1968

PROTEST SIGN

The "I Am a Man" protest sign was created for the Memphis sanitation strike after two workers were crushed to death in the back of their garbage truck. The slogan, a response to a nineteenth-century abolitionist poster that asked "Am I not a man?" emerged as a unifying theme. The single color of scarlet red and raw printing demonstrate the immediacy of the cause.

Salmon

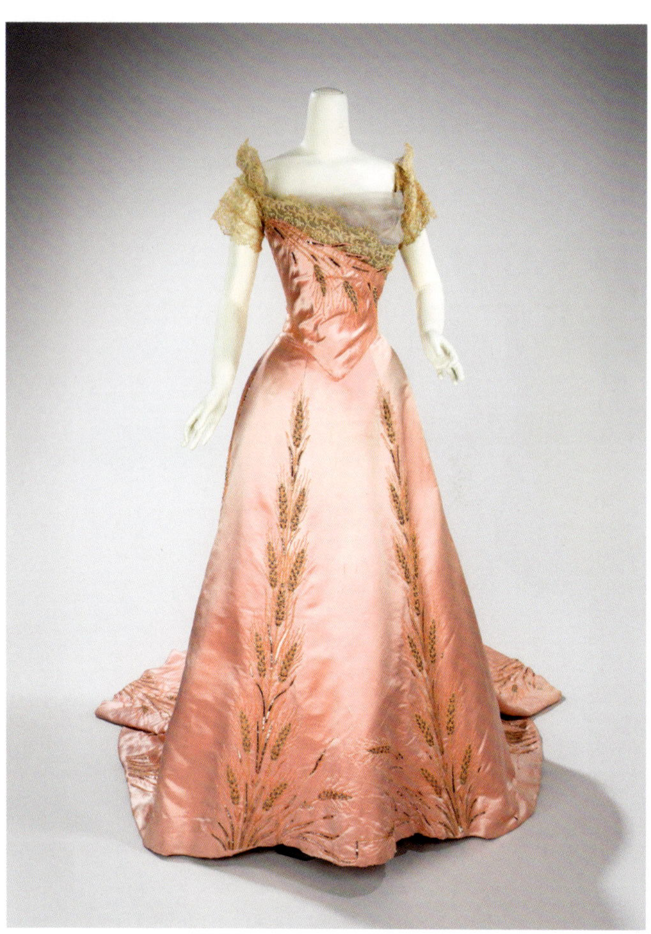

14

Ball Gown, House of Worth

Jean-Philippe Worth ~ 1900

GOWN

Jean-Philippe Worth became the lead designer for the House of Worth in 1895. He was renowned for designing elaborate and dazzling gowns with intricate trimmings on unique textiles in subtle shades of cream, pink, and salmon. These delicate colors required handcrafting, the best—and often most expensive—materials, and extreme care to produce.

WARM COLORS

Carnation

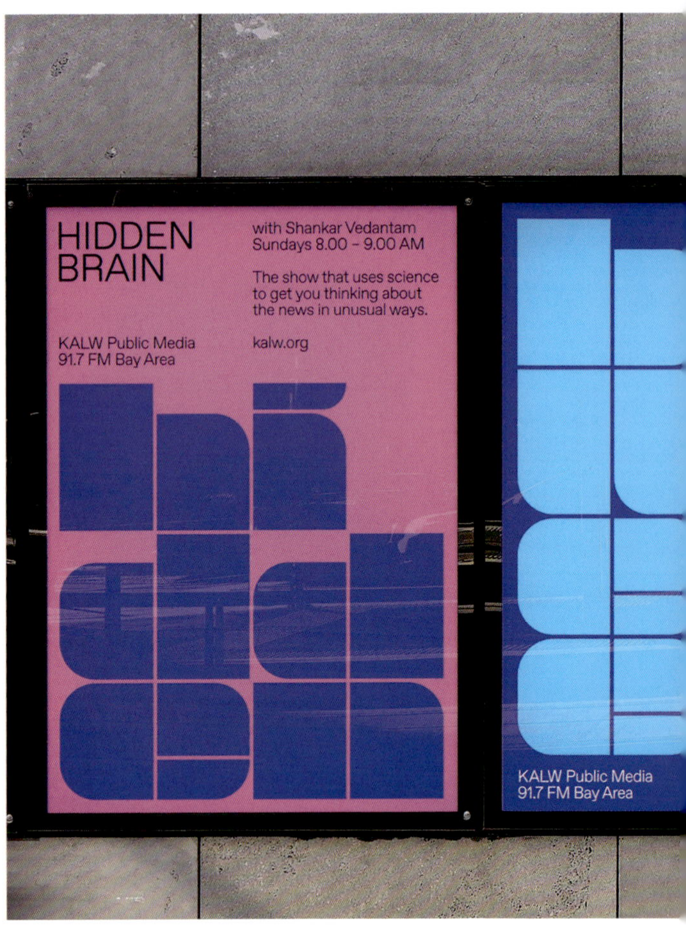

15

KALW Public Media

Collins ~ 2023

BRANDING

For the venerable San Francisco radio station, KALW, the design team at Collins created a symbol as powerful as KALW's content to express the station's vibrant future. Relying on type, intense color, and abstract letterforms, the branding references the simplicity of jazz and classical concert posters from the 1950s and 1960s. The ultrabright color palette demands attention and expresses KALW's less-than-traditional attitude.

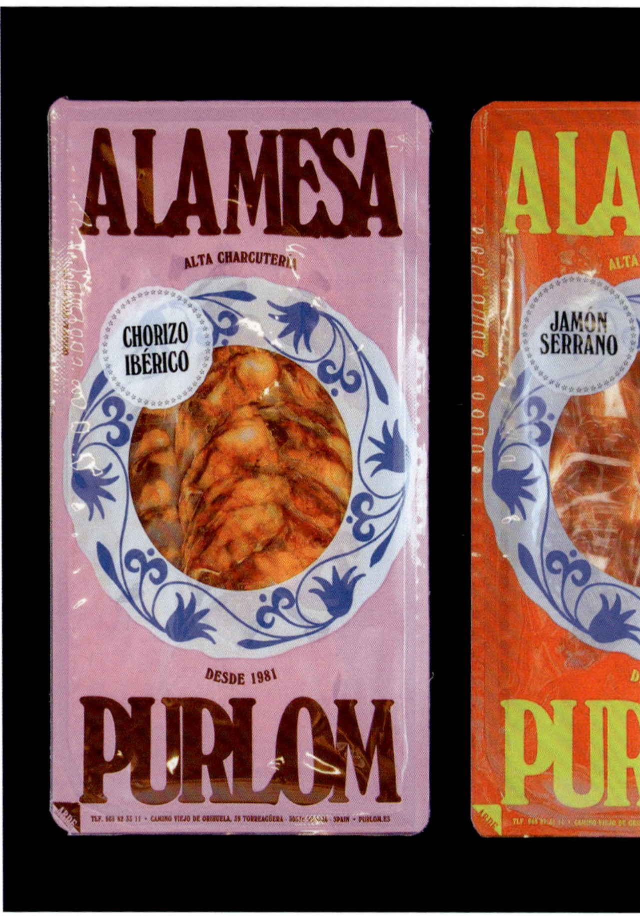

16

Purlom A La Mesa

Onmi Design ~ 2023

PACKAGING

For the charcuterie brand PURLOM, Onmi Design created packaging with nostalgia and an expressive personality. The unique box design fits all products, each one a lively color. To appeal to a younger audience without alienating the traditional longtime buyer, Onmi merged time-honored motifs, such as the decorative plate, with playful typography and a nostalgic palette—for this product: pink, plum, blue, and white.

Magenta

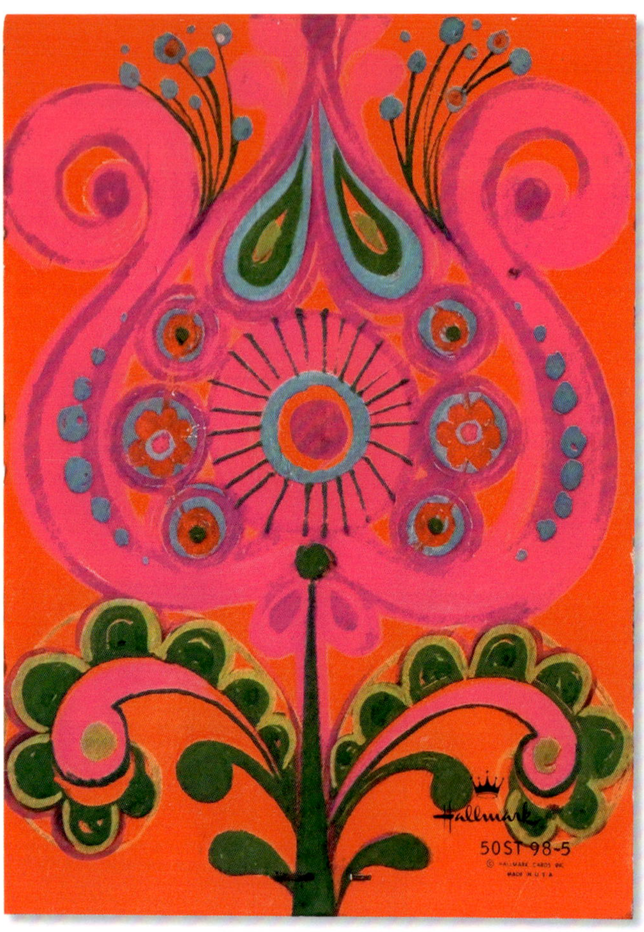

17

Paisley Notepad

Hallmark Cards ~ 1972

NOTEPAD

By the 1970s, the expressive and rebellious colors of the Fillmore poster movement began to appear in mainstream advertising and branding. Initially associated with psychedelic drugs and optical art, intense combinations such as red, orange, green, and magenta signified a youthful and fresh attitude. This notebook was described as "now" and, "of the moment, part of a new energy."

WARM COLORS

Violet

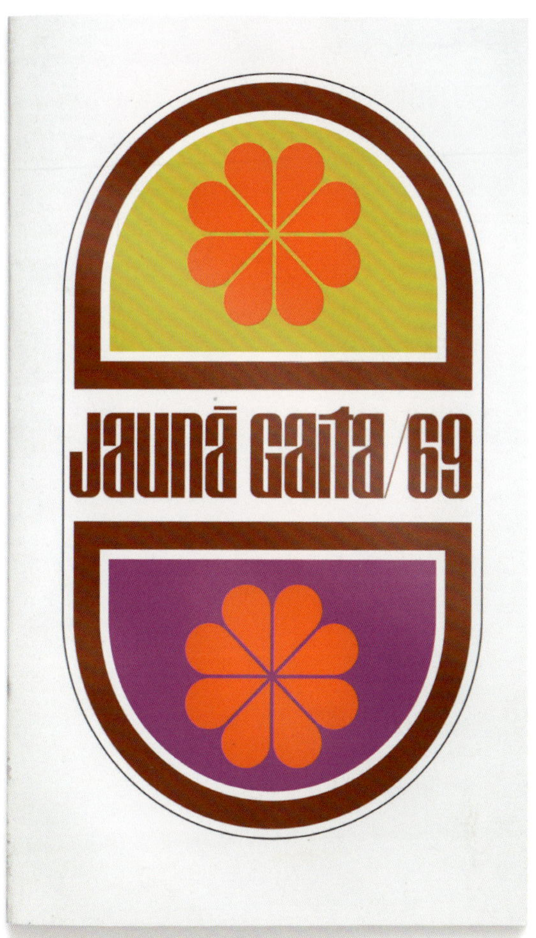

18

Jaunā Gaita 69

Ilmārs Rumpēters ~ 1968

MAGAZINE COVER

After the Second World War many Latvian writers relocated to Great Britain, Canada, and the United States. They began their own periodicals, including *Jaunā Gaita* (*The New Course*). Designer Ilmārs Rumpēters captured ideas of modernism and expression with different covers for each issue. The variety of colors matched the breadth of ideas. One issue might be bright with violet and ocher, and another gray, black, and white.

Lavender

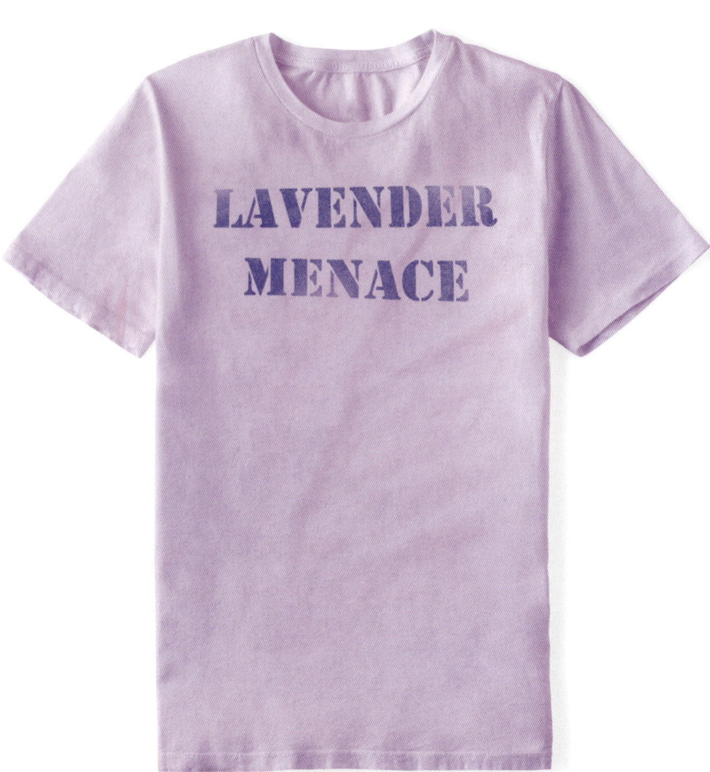

19

Lavender Menace

Lesbian Liberation ~ 1970

T-SHIRT

In 1969, Betty Friedan, president of the National Organization for Women (NOW) used the term "lavender menace" to express concern about the negative influence of outspoken lesbians on the women's movement. At the time "lavender" was a popular slang term used for gay men. Rita Mae Brown and members of the lesbian liberation movement adopted the term, wearing the T-shirt as a protest at the Second Congress to Unite Women.

Periwinkle

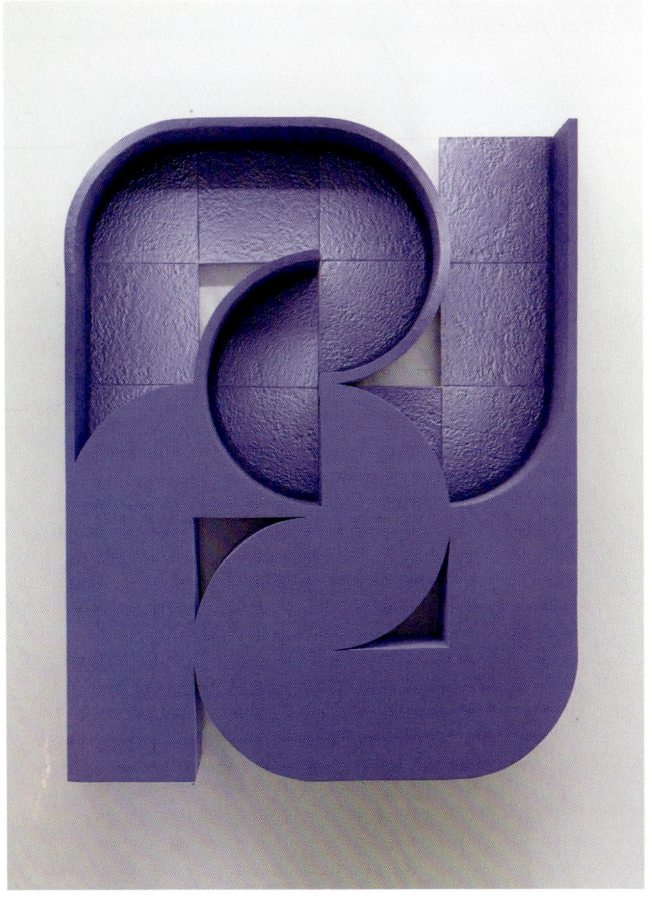

20

Rational Design

Amir Nikravan ~ 2018

SCULPTURE

Amir Nikravan's sculptures are informed by the history of Los Angeles' architecture, from the Case Study House program to the public buildings of Edward Durell Stone, and the vernacular styles and DIY finishes of the anonymous—frequently immigrant—homeowners. Nikravan explores form as a facade for meaning, and its effect on our understanding of architecture, design, surface, color, and shape.

Lilac

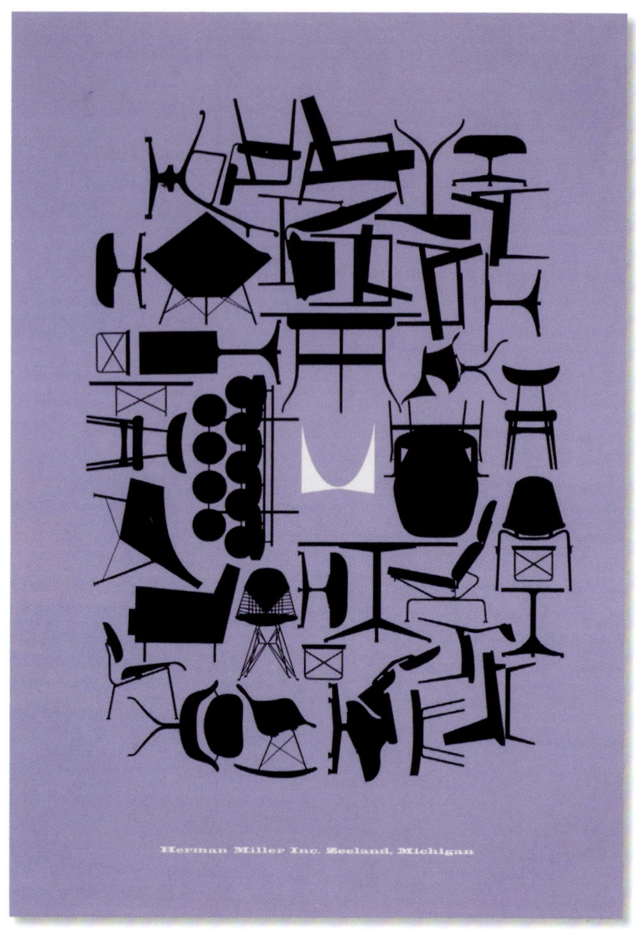

21

Herman Miller Inc.

Don Ervin ~ 1961

ADVERTISEMENT

Don Ervin was a master of logo design, with commissions from Conoco, MetLife, Transamerica, Cargill, Abbott Laboratories, and TRW, among others. This ad for Herman Miller furniture displays Ervin's skill in combining the forms of iconic designs and color. It features an assemblage of black silhouettes of tables and chairs against a periwinkle background with the company's logo in white.

Purple

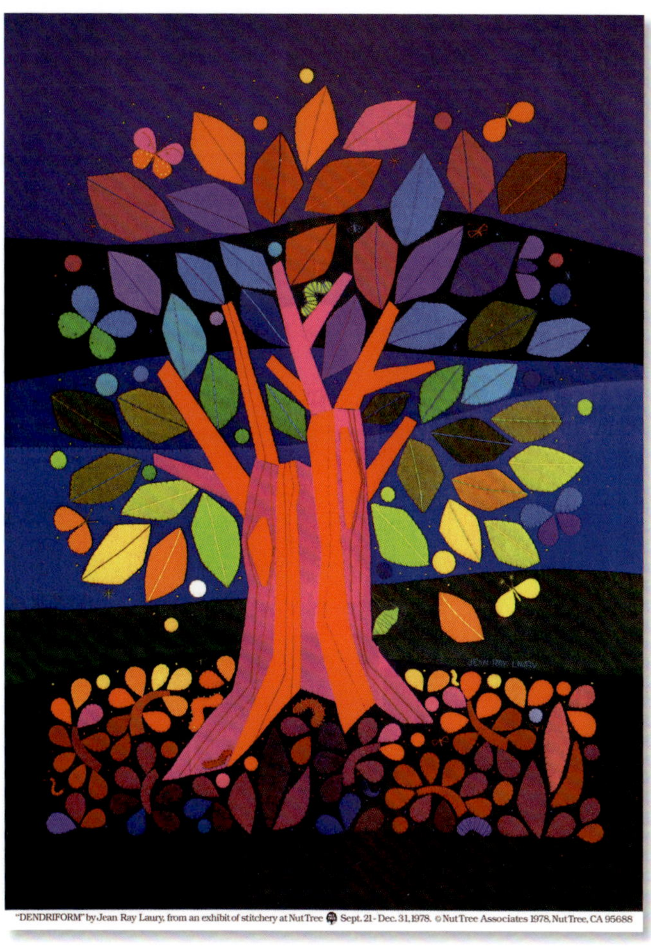

22

Dendriform

Jean Ray Laury ~ 1978

QUILT ON POSTER

Jean Ray Laury shifted quilting as a medium from craft to fine art. Instead of creating conventional quilts with pattern, Laury treated fabric as "paint." The works often incorporated humor and commentary. Here, Laury created a multicolored tree that leaps from the deep purple background. It explores concepts of growth, connection, life, and renewal. The leaves may be many colors and shapes, but they share the same source.

Royal Blue

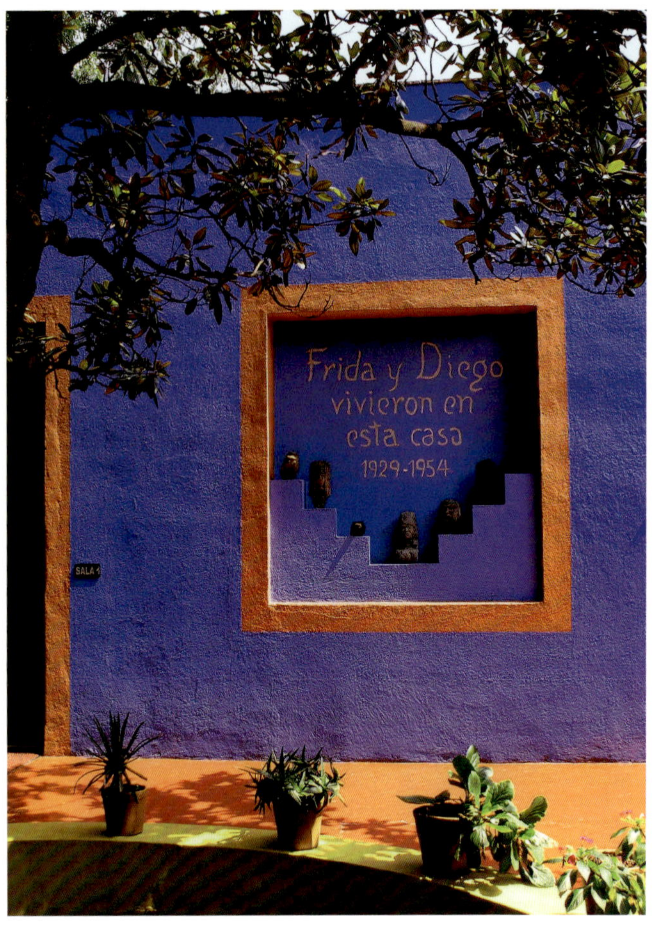

23

La Casa Azul, Mexico City

Frida Kahlo ~ 1907–54

ARCHITECTURE

Frida Kahlo was born in La Casa Azul in 1907. It remained her home throughout her life. Kahlo and her husband Diego Rivera painted the house royal blue to represent her admiration for Mexico's indigenous people and to honor their craft and culture. In Mexican folklore, blue is associated with spirituality and protection. The royal blue color created a sense of sanctuary for Kahlo during many years of ill health.

COOL COLORS

Midnight Blue

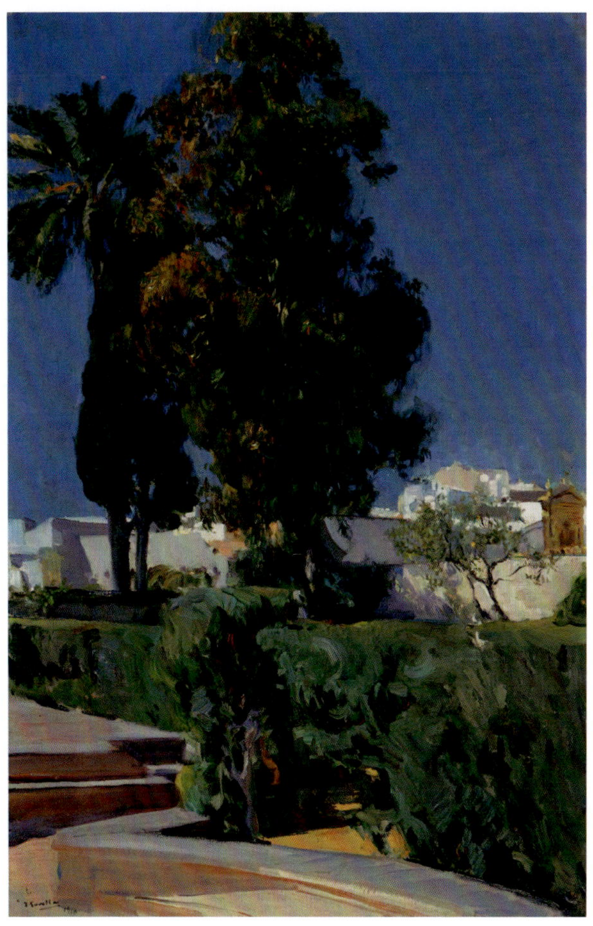

24

Corner of the Garden, Alcazar, Sevilla

Joaquín Sorolla y Bastida ~ 1910

PAINTING

Joaquín Sorolla y Bastida's painting of the garden at Seville's Alcázar (palace) in Spain displays his concentration on proportion, form, and the light of the country's southern region. Unlike other works, which explored a changing dynamic of light and reflections, this painting has a sense of stillness due to the midnight blue sky, simplified forms of the buildings and plantings, and absence of people.

Navy

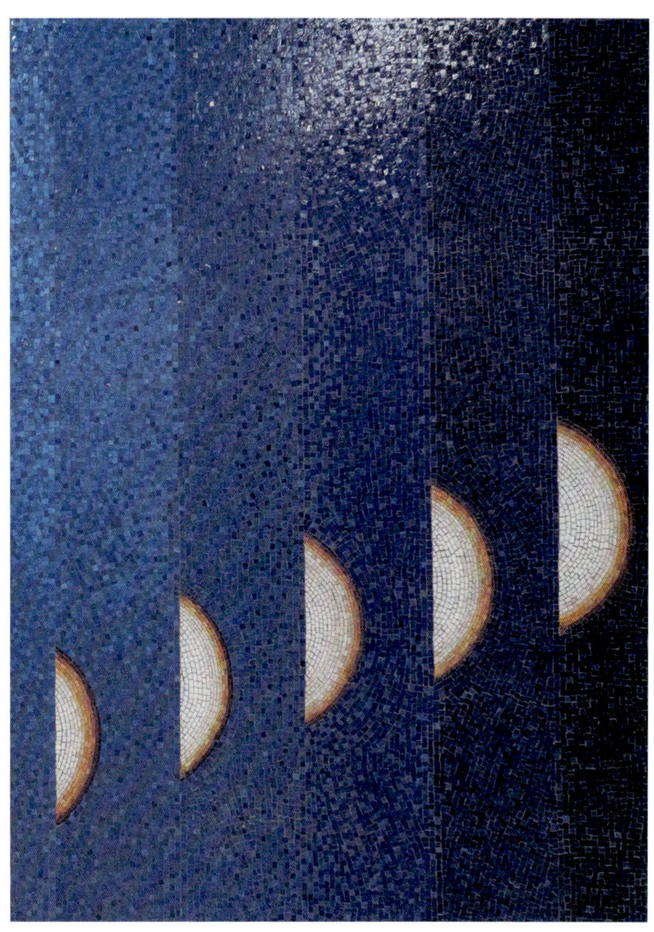

25

At The Same Time (section)

Rebeca Méndez Studio ~ 2019

MURAL

"No matter how idiosyncratic our neighborhoods are, we share something in common," says Rebeca Méndez. Working with thousands of photos of the Los Angeles sky, Méndez's mural displays the complexity of the clouds and shades of blue through the day. For her, the sky became a metaphor for the diversity of the people in Los Angeles: "It is constantly changing, and it's constantly becoming other."

Blue

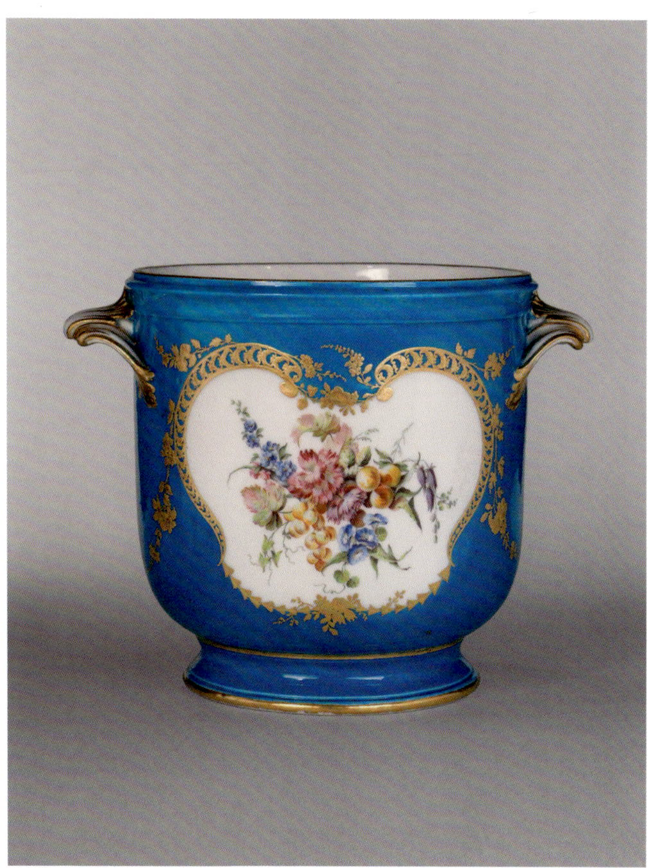

26

Bottle Cooler from the Louis XV Service

Jean-Claude Duplessis ~ 1754

POTTERY

Produced by the Vincennes porcelain manufactory, this bottle cooler was part of a service for French King Louis XV. *Bleu céleste* (heavenly blue) was the most expensive and difficult color to produce due to the labor required and scarcity of glazing material. The factory's chemist, Jean Hellot, described it as "the royal blue or turquoise blue of the complete service of His Majesty found in 1753 by me."

Cardinal Blue

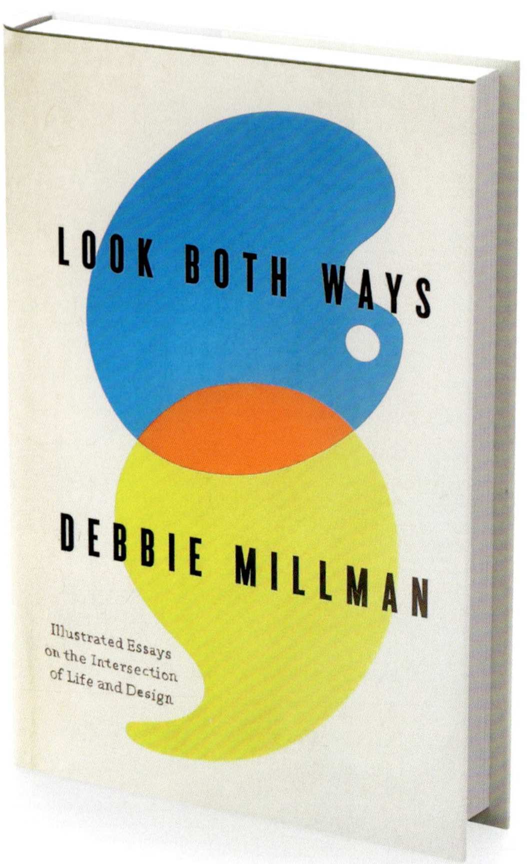

27

Look Both Ways

Debbie Millman and Rodrigo Corral ~ 2009

BOOK

In *Look Both Ways*, branding consultant and design leader Debbie Millman presents a collection of essays that explore the deep connection between design and everyday life. The content touches on the personal, professional, and universal, and finding their intersections. The cover combines a paint palette and speech bubble. If the viewer flips the book, the cardinal blue palette becomes a face with an orange brain, thus reinforcing the title.

COOL COLORS

Sky Blue

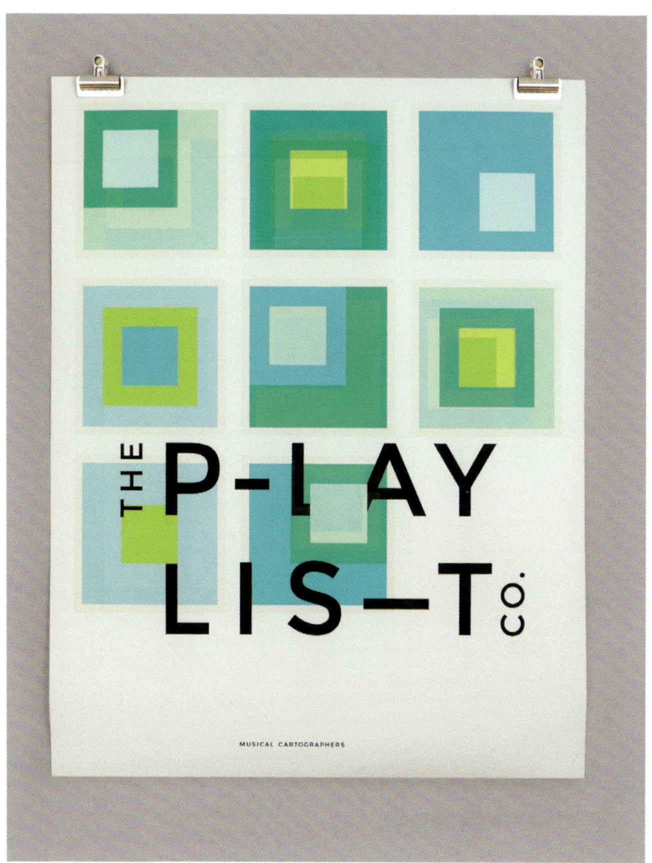

28

The Playlist Company

Blok Design ~ 2023

POSTER

The Playlist Company is known for its musical expertise across genres and eras, creating sonic experiences for Canadian hospitality brands. Blok Design's poster reflects a musical quality that suggests movement with a palette of cool tones: sky blue, mint, seafoam, turquoise, lime green, and others. The layers of color in multiple positions within a square create the sense of movement and music.

COOL COLORS

Ice Blue

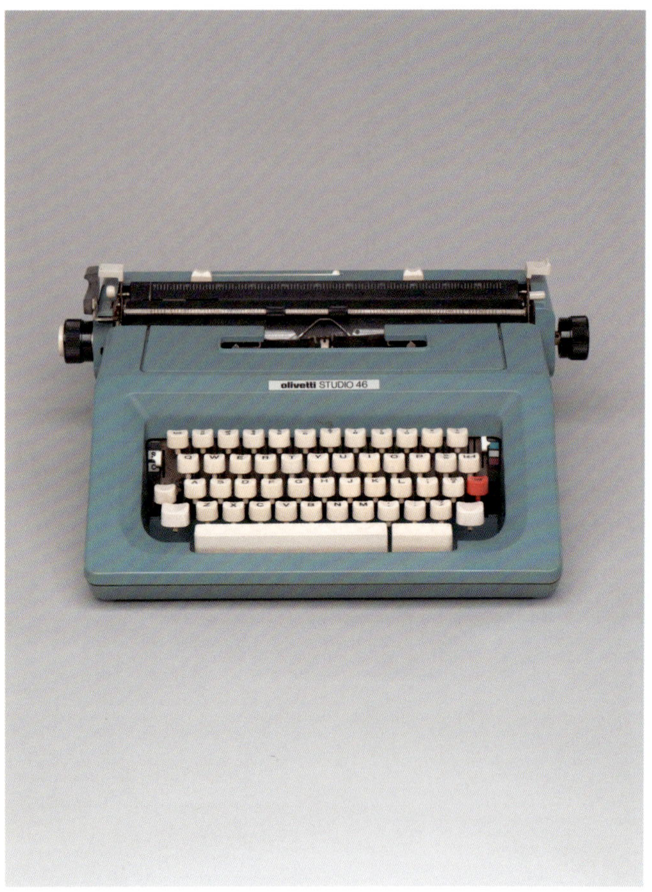

29

Olivetti Studio 46 Typewriter

Used by author Octavia E. Butler ~ ca. 1977

TYPEWRITER

This Olivetti Studio 46 typewriter belonged to noted author Octavia E. Butler, one of the twentieth century's greatest science-fiction writers. Butler's manual blue typewriter dates to the mid-1970s. Olivetti designed the ice blue case with a red "tab" key in a field of creamy white. The typewriter was featured in the Smithsonian exhibition, "All the Stories Are True: African American Writers Speak."

COOL COLORS

Seafoam

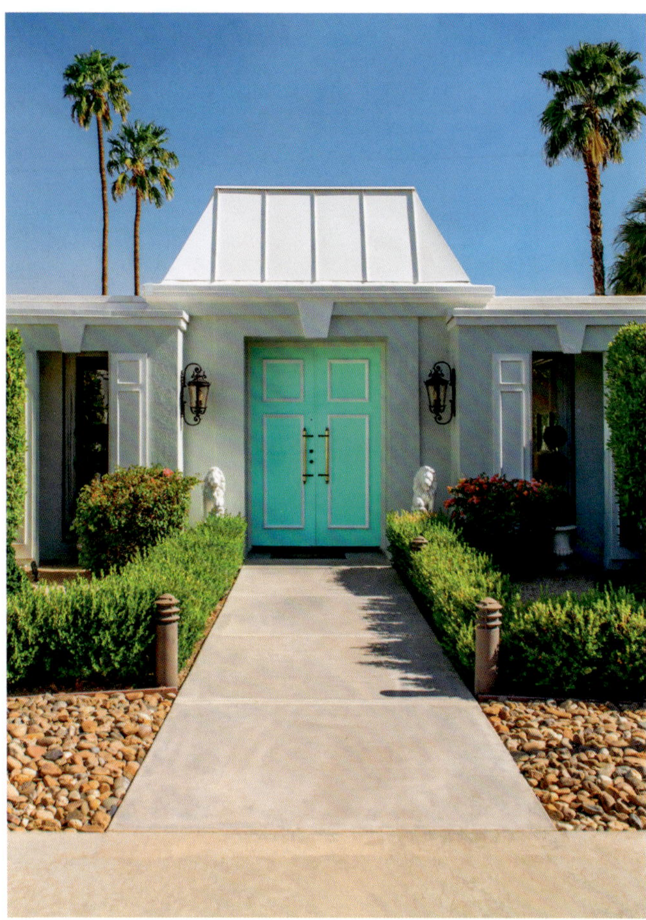

30

Wheatley House, Palm Springs

James McNaughton and Hal Lacy ~ 1972

ARCHITECTURE

The Wheatley House is an excellent example of the Hollywood Regency style, with a mansard roof over a symmetrical entry court and double doors. Hollywood Regency, first used by Hollywood set designers in the 1930s, mixed multiple styles for a cinematic effect. Set in a neighborhood known for its brightly colored entry doors, those at Wheatley House are painted seafoam blue and accentuated by gold door handles.

COOL COLORS

Mint

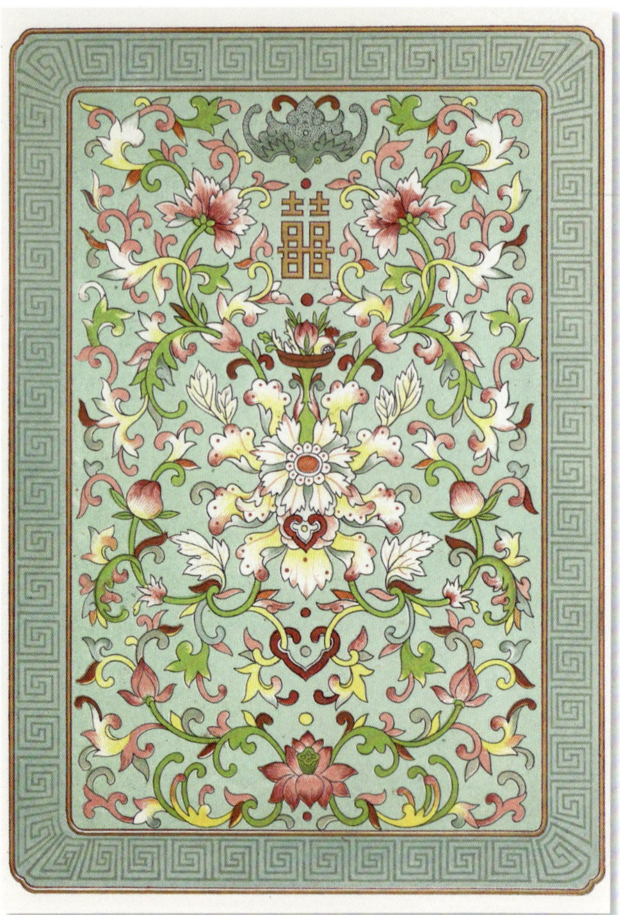

31

Examples of Chinese Ornament

Owen Jones ~ 1867

BOOK

During political tumult in nineteenth-century China, many of the best examples of artworks from the Ming, Qing, and earlier dynasties, were sold to Western collectors. Architect Owen Jones, who also wrote *The Grammar of Ornament* (1856), pioneered a new technology of chromolithography with his own press. The process allowed him to reproduce the precise colors and gilding in *Examples of Chinese Ornament.*

Turquoise

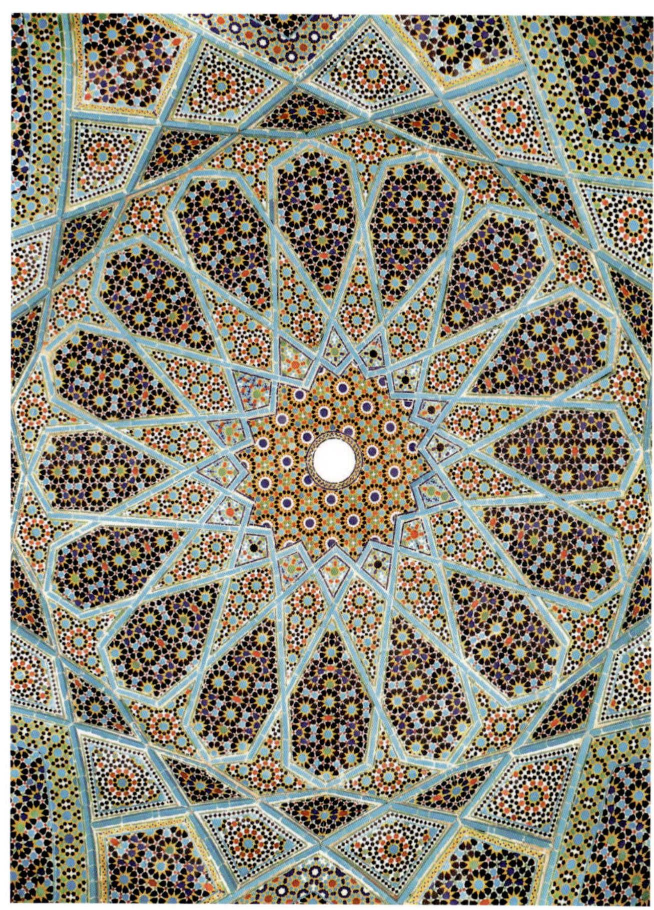

32

Enamel Tile, Tomb of Hafez

André Godard ~ 1935

TILE

This enameled-tile mosaic on the ceiling of the pavilion at the Tomb of Hafez in Iran incorporates traditional forms of Islamic architectural details. With a prohibition on representative figural imagery, Islamic ornament is rich with complex geometric tile patterns. The color turquoise signifies the impenetrable depths of the universe.

COOL COLORS

Peacock Green

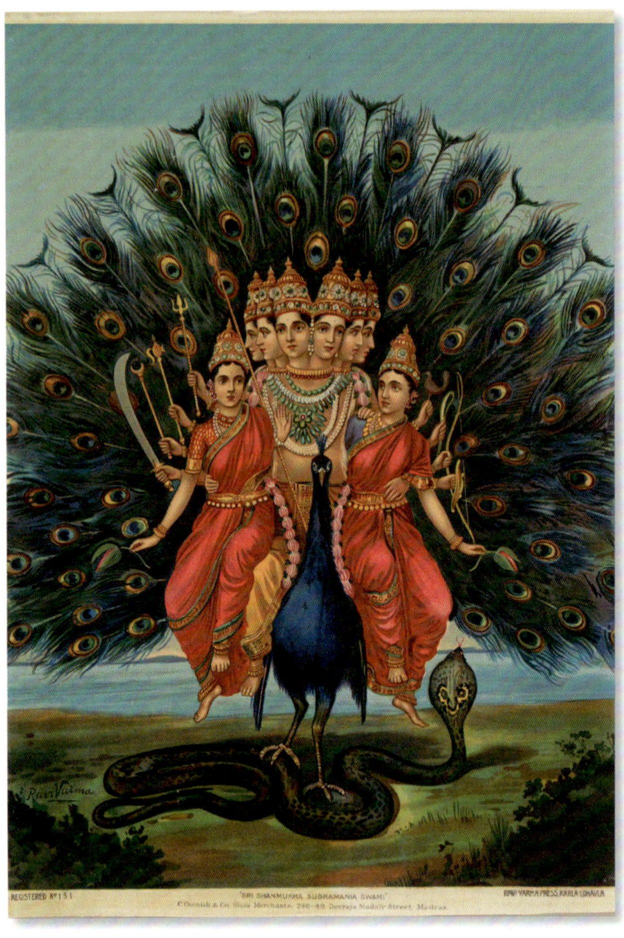

33

Shri Shanmukha Subramania Swami

Unknown ~ ca. 1900–15

LITHOGRAPHIC PRINT

This Indian print depicts Skanda (Subramania), the god of war. His name translates as "jumping," an action associated with both young men in combat and with the peacock, which Skanda is often shown riding. Skanda is accompanied by his wives from north and south India to emphasize his universality. The peacock, and peacock green, are symbols of India and metaphors of Skanda's power to destroy ignorance and evil.

Teal

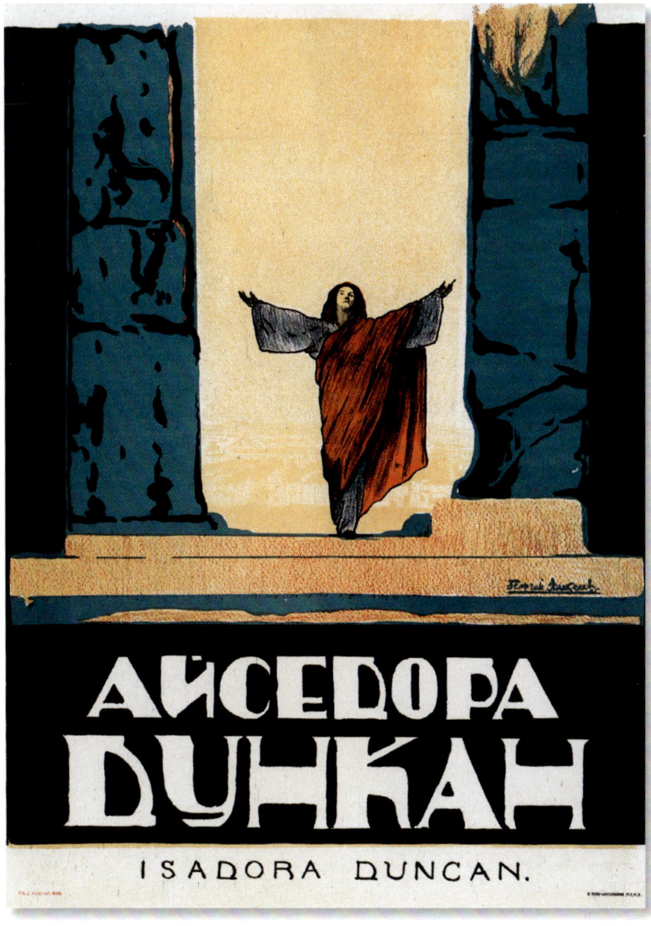

34

Isadora Duncan

Georgi Alexeiev ~ 1921

POSTER

Georgi Alexeiev was a passionate and acclaimed propaganda artist in the Soviet Union. He worked as a painter, sculptor, and graphic artist, fully committed to Marxist-Leninist concepts of socialism. The poster for a performance by the modernist dancer Isadora Duncan depicts her as a classical Greek goddess. Here, Alexeiev uses red to symbolize the Soviet Union's emergence from the dark teal canyon of history.

British Racing Green

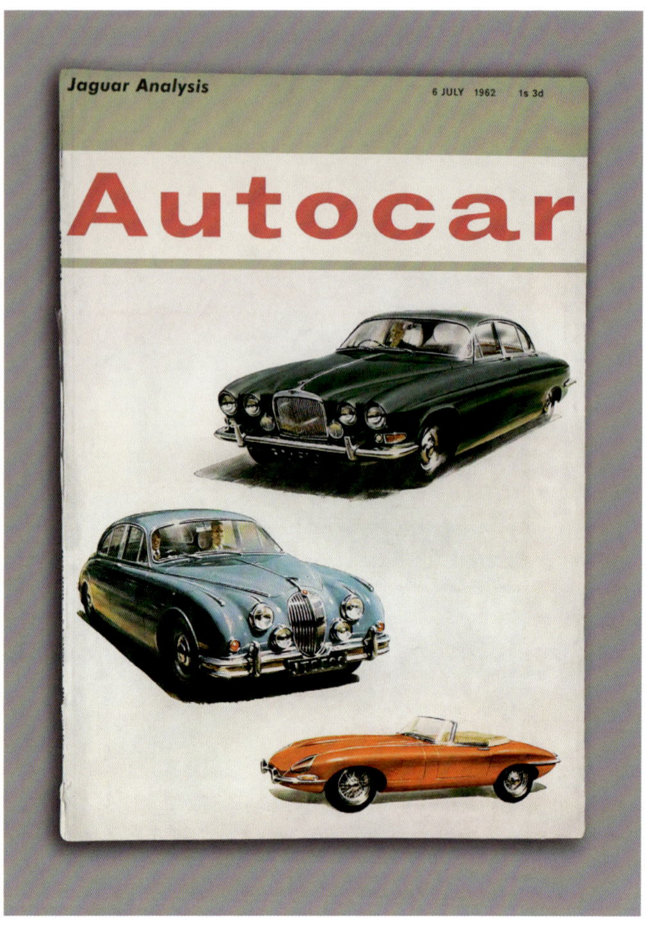
Jaguar Analysis
6 JULY 1962
1s 3d
Autocar

35

Autocar: Jaguar Analysis

Unknown ~ 1962

MAGAZINE COVER

There is no exact color of British Racing Green. It varies in shade and tone with each automobile company. However, the green here is the most consistent application. In 1903, Great Britain hosted the Gordon Bennett Cup. Unfortunately, due to England's snail's pace speed limit of 12 miles per hour, the organizers moved the race to Ireland. British racers painted their cars green in homage to the Emerald Isle for hosting the race.

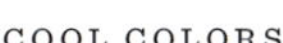

COOL COLORS

Forest

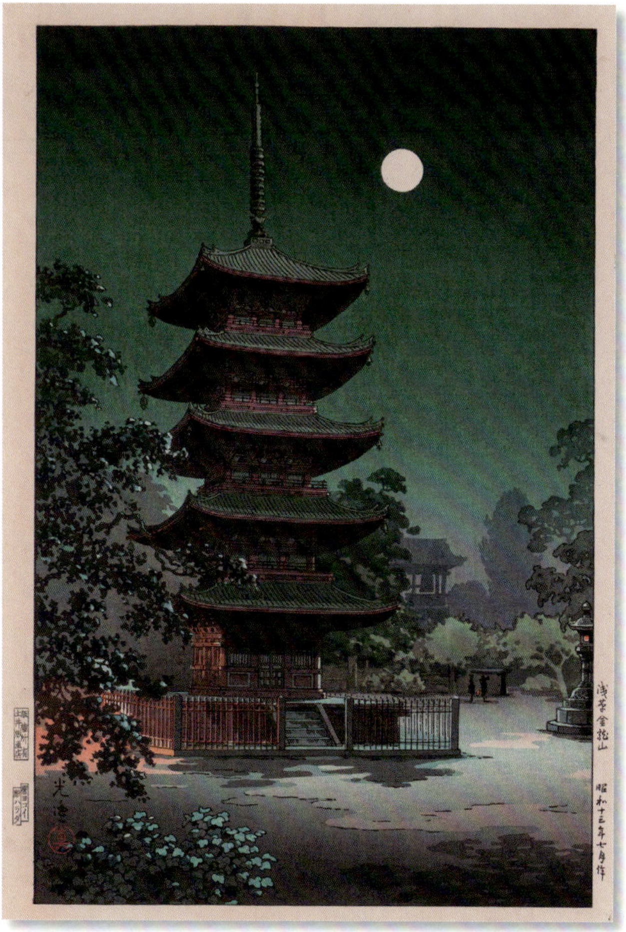

36

Sketches of Famous Places in Japan: Asakusa Kinryūzan Temple

Tsuchiya Kōitsu ~ 1938

COLOR WOODCUT

Tsuchiya Kōitsu worked with a style of woodcut, *shin hanga*, meaning new prints. The style, aimed at European and American markets, presented a nostalgic and romanticized depiction of Japan. The style incorporates some of the Impressionist ideas of painting light. Kōitsu printed multiple layers of color to capture the deep forest green while maintaining the delicate blue leaves in the foreground.

Emerald Green

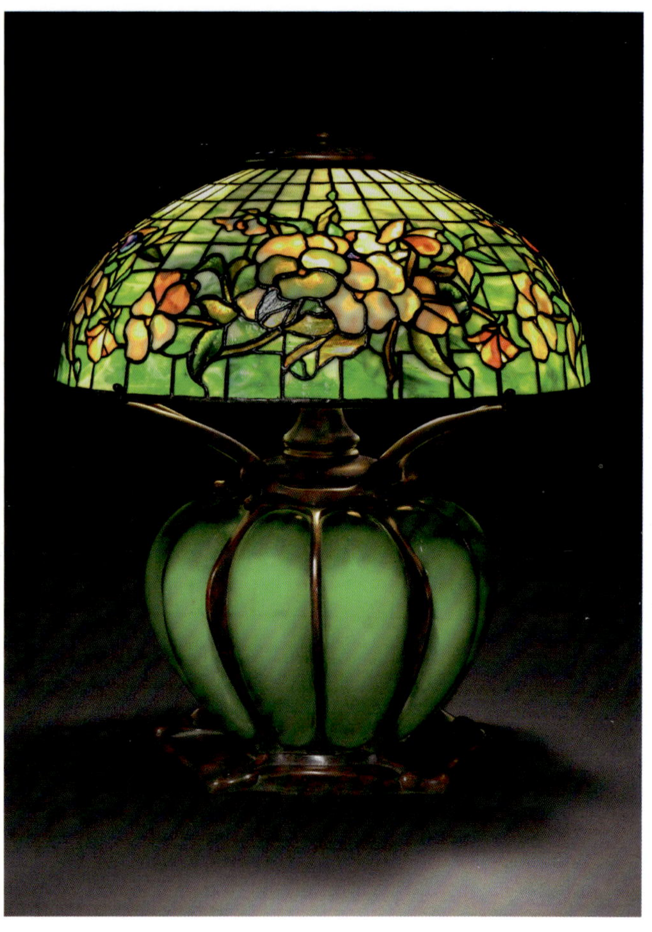

37

Pansy Border Table Lamp

Clara Wolcott Driscoll (attributed) ~ ca. 1902–10

LAMP

Clara Wolcott Driscoll likely designed the Pansy Border table lamp, inspired by the emerald-green, yellow, and red garden flowers of spring. The Tiffany lamp features a unique base where green glass is blown into a bronze cage, a challenging technique because glass and bronze cool at different temperatures. If not handled correctly, the glass will shatter.

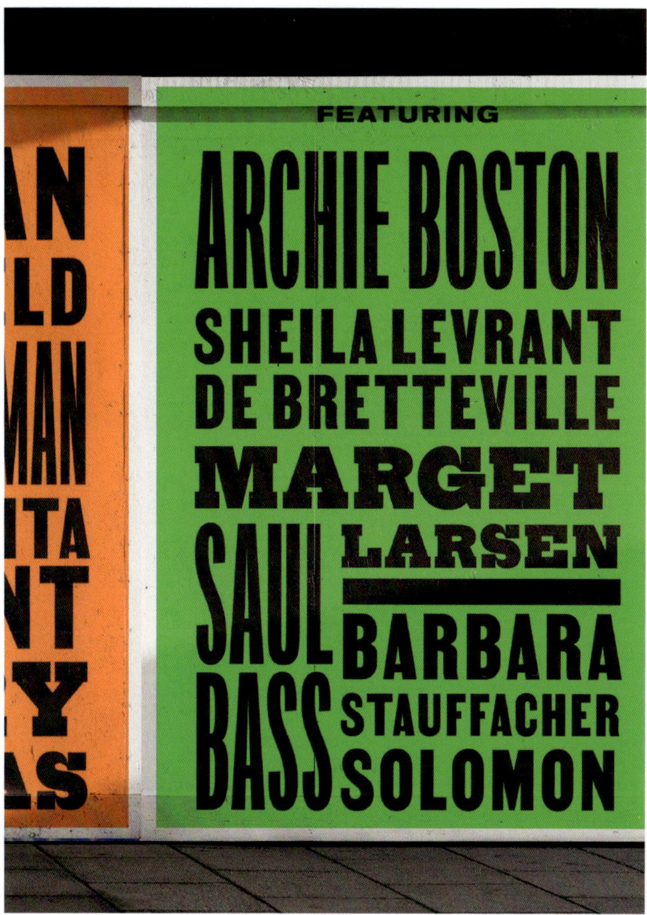

38

Surf Sun Sand Serif

Brian White ~ 2023

GRAPHIC IDENTITY

Surf Sun Sand Serif celebrates the designers who influenced West Coast culture through their creativity. The visual language features a vibrant color palette, with green serving as the unifying element across all applications. The multiple colors and letterpress typography reflect California's design aesthetic and draws inspiration from iconic posters and broadsides common in Los Angeles.

COOL COLORS

Kelly Green

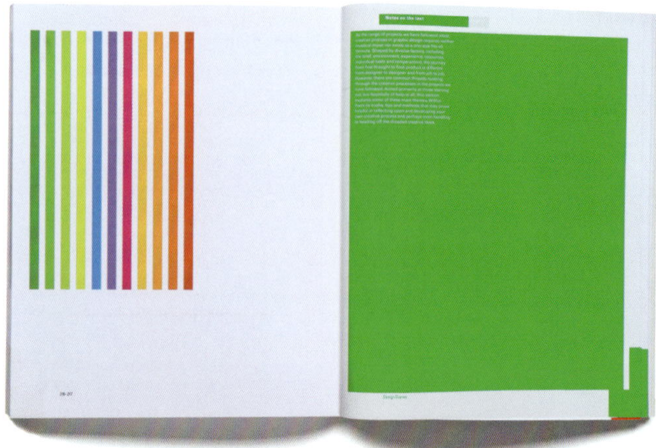

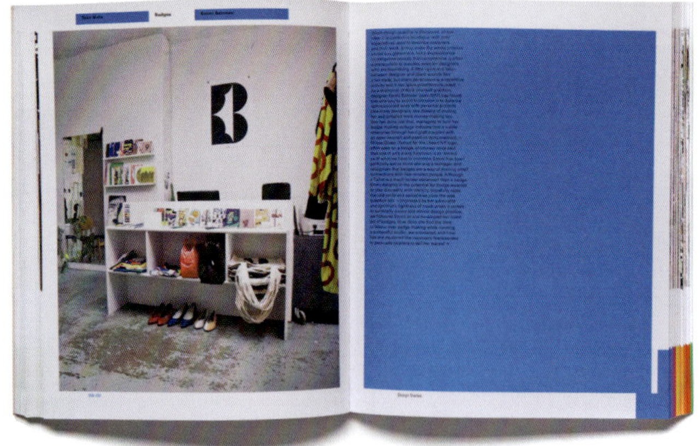

39

Design Diaries: Creative Process in Graphic Design

Lucienne Roberts+ ~ 2010

BOOK

For *Design Diaries,* Lucienne Roberts employed bright, rainbow colors and bold, flat shapes with documentary-style images to enhance the reading experience. The result is a remarkable book following projects through the design process from the first pitch and initial concept to the final product, accompanied by commentary from the designers of each project.

COOL COLORS

Tea Green

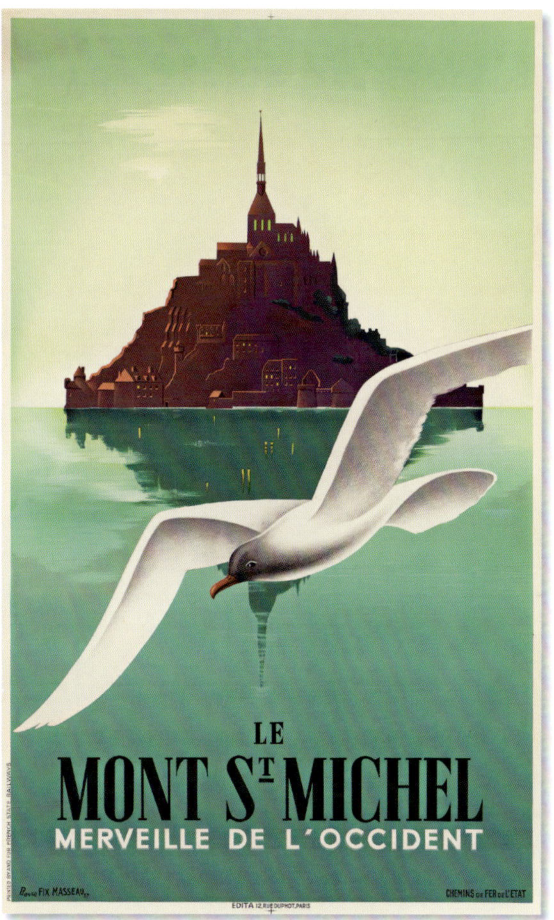

40

Le Mont St Michel, Merveille de l'Occident

Pierre Fix-Masseau ~ 1937

POSTER

Pierre Fix-Masseau was a notable poster designer in the 1930s, celebrated for his masterful use of color, shape, and scale. This dynamic poster features a tea-green sky, creating a halo behind the brown silhouette of Mont St. Michel and a white seagull. Fix-Masseau's artistic philosophy emphasized simplicity, directness, and a universal language, making his style a perfect fit for the poster medium.

Lime Green

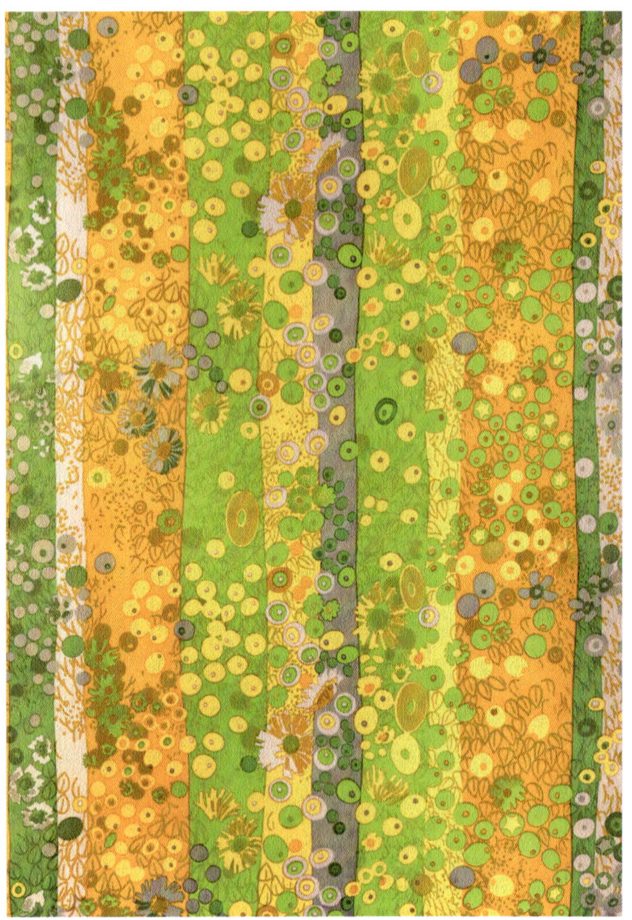

41

Primavera

Don Wight and Larsen Design Studio ~ 1959

TEXTILE

Primavera was the first printed velvet produced by the Larsen Design Studio in 1959. Wight and Larsen drew inspiration from the paintings of Gustav Klimt and the Dunhuang murals in Gansu Province, China. The lime green, periwinkle, and chartreuse tones of Primavera closely relate to the malachite and azurite pigments found in many of the dazzling Dunhuang murals.

Chartreuse

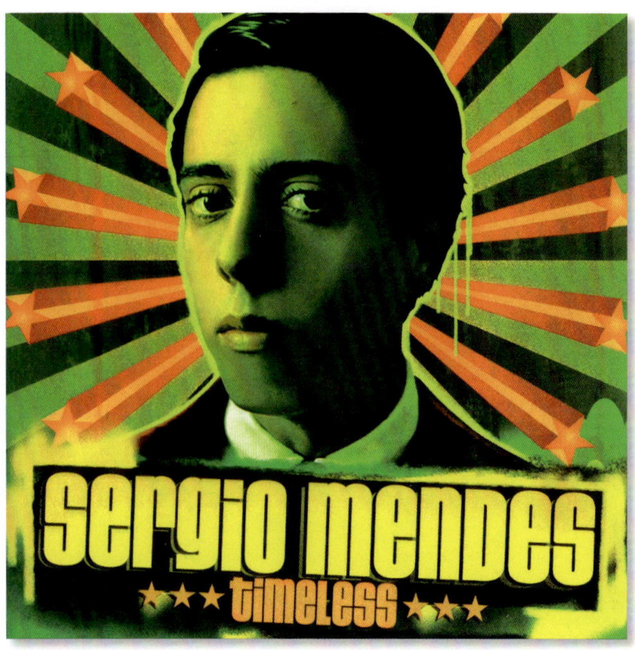

42

Sérgio Mendes, Timeless

Roland Young ~ 2006

ALBUM COVER

For his album *Timeless*, legendary Brazilian Sérgio Mendes collaborated with the Black Eyed Peas' will.i.am and others, including Erykah Badu, Justin Timberlake, Jill Scott, and Black Thought. Roland Young's design incorporated Mendes's portrait from his 1966 album, *The Swinger From Rio.* Here, however, Young applies a bright chartreuse color and streaming stars in the background to communicate the vitality of the new content.

EARTH COLORS

Avocado

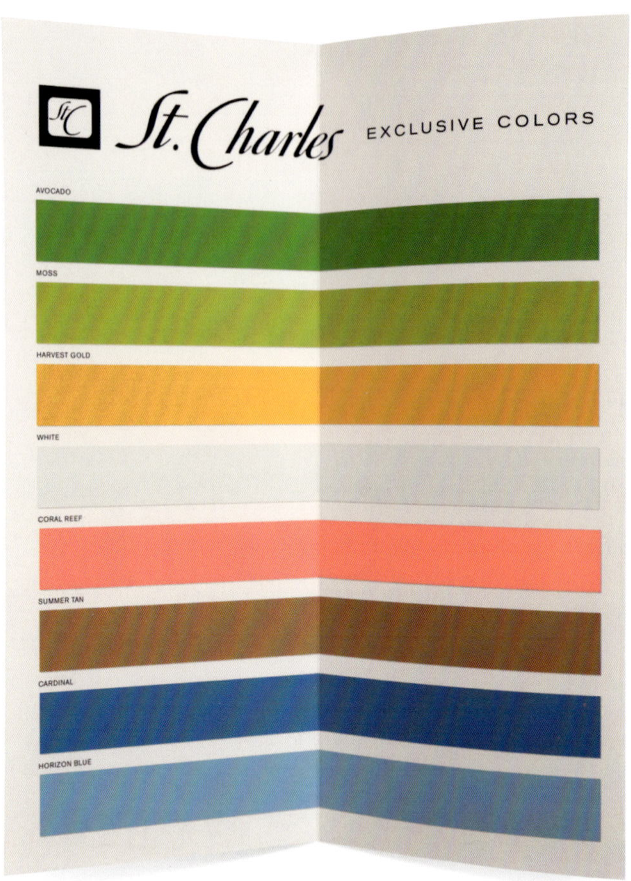

43

St. Charles Exclusive Colors

Unknown ~ 1964

PAINT PALETTE

By the 1960s, the postwar desire for pastel colors—which had reflected 1950s optimism and the need for calm after the Depression and Second World War—waned. The public began to turn to deeper colors and jewel tones. The St. Charles palette shows this shift, and introduces early examples of Avocado, Moss, and Harvest Gold. These colors became synonymous with the 1970s environmentalist movement.

EARTH COLORS

Pistachio

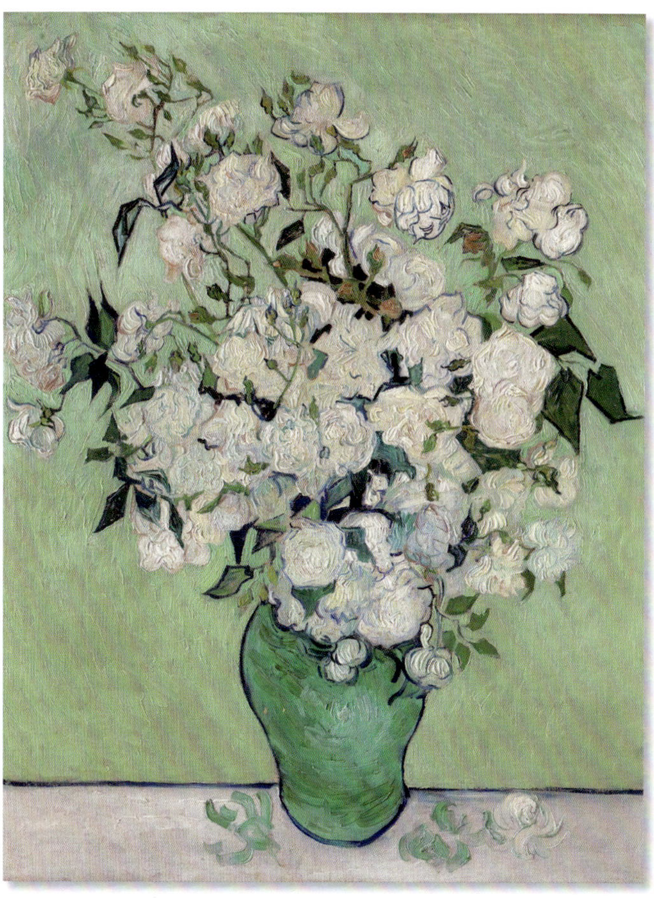

44

Roses

Vincent van Gogh ~ 1890

PAINTING

The day before his departure from the asylum in Saint-Rémy, France, Vincent van Gogh painted *Roses*. The paint colors have faded over time; what was once vibrant green has turned to a more muted pistachio. Van Gogh viewed green as a symbol of birth and renewal. The roses in the painting were originally pink, not white, creating a striking contrast with the complementary green background.

EARTH COLORS

Eucalyptus

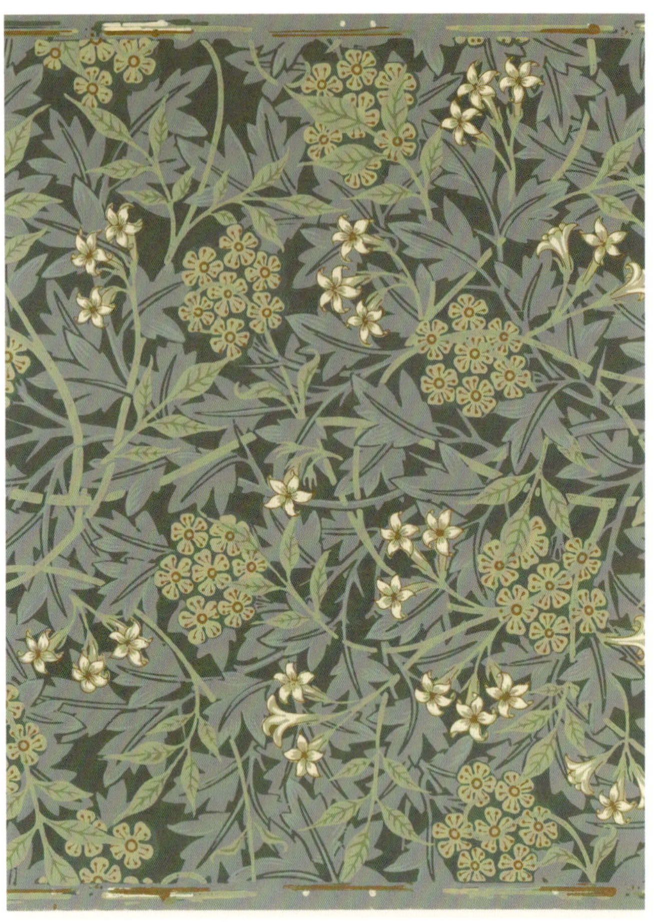

45

Jasmine

William Morris ~ 1872

WALLPAPER

First produced in 1872, Morris's "Jasmine" wallpaper features a pattern of hawthorn leaves and blossoms, intricately designed with scrolling jasmine. Each color was printed separately, with wallpaper designs using anything from twenty to sixty-eight different colors. This meticulous, handcrafted process, lasting up to four weeks for a single design, reflects Morris's rejection of the mass production of the industrial era.

Olive Green

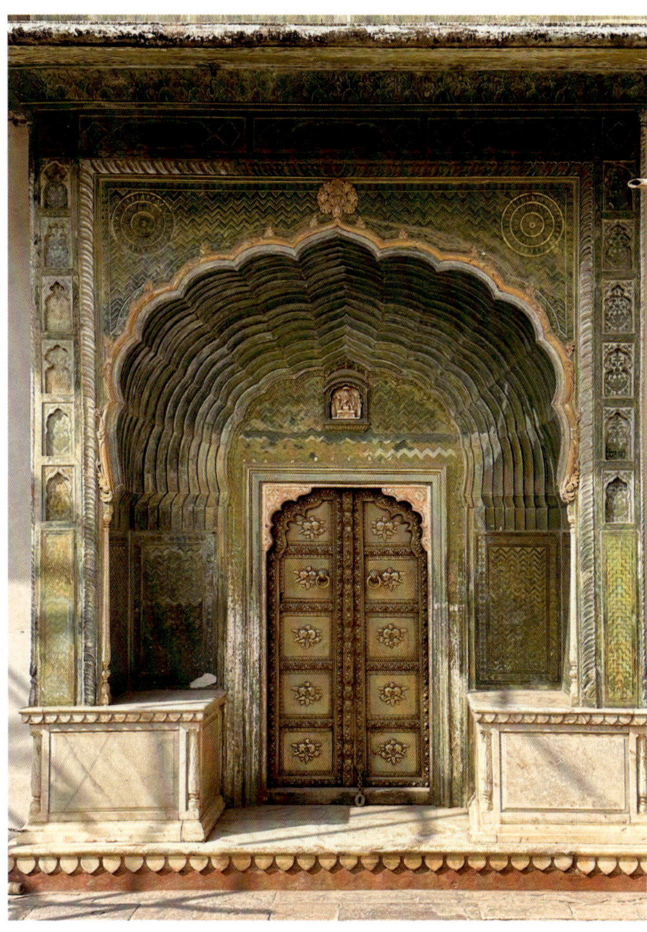

46

Leheriya Gate, Pritam Niwas Chowk, Jaipur City Palace

Vidyadhar Bhattacharya ~ 1729–32

ARCHITECTURE

Built by Maharaja Sawai Jai Singh II, the City Palace was designed to create harmonious living spaces that promoted well-being, prosperity, and happiness. The palace includes several buildings, gardens, and temples. Four small gates (known as Ridhi Sidhi Pol) each represent a season and Hindu god in the inner courtyard. The exquisite wave forms in olive green of the Leheriya Gate represent Spring and Lord Ganesha.

EARTH COLORS

Khaki Green

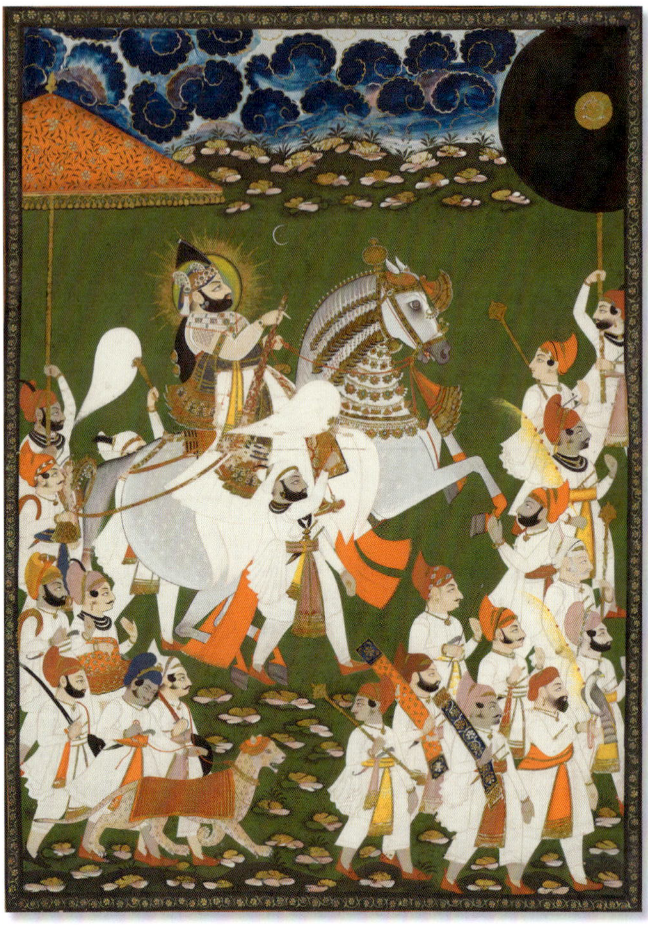

47

Maharana Bhim Singh in Procession

Ghasi (attributed) ~ ca. 1820

PAINTING

In this royal procession, Mewari ruler Maharana Bhim Singh rides through Mewar, India, displaying power and comfort. Adorned with jewels and tattoos, he holds the reins of his horse and a hookah mouthpiece. Surrounding him on a khaki green field is an entourage that includes men carrying royal standards, a leashed cheetah, and a falcon. He proudly showcases the insignia of his clan—a black solar disk with a gold sun.

Moss

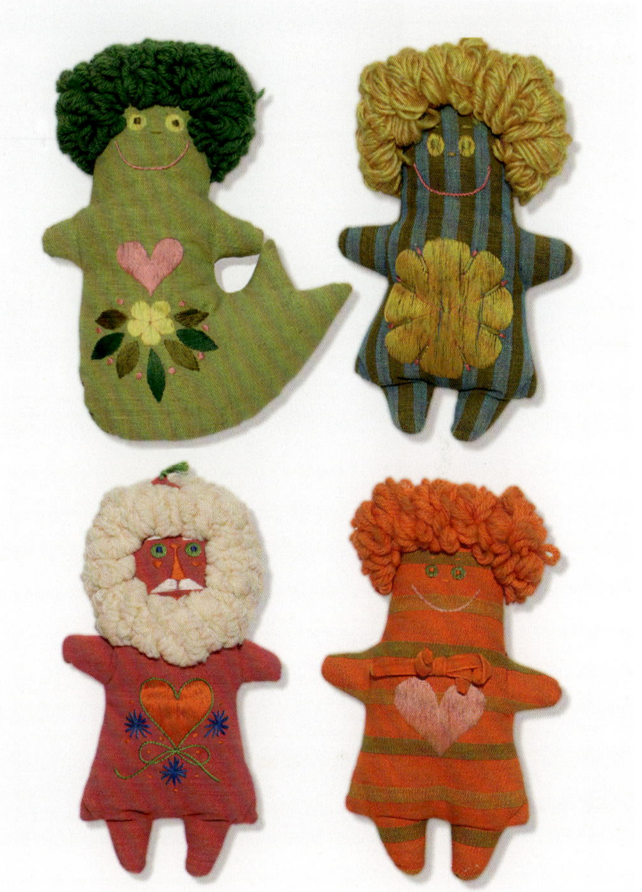

48

Dolls

Marilyn Neuhart ~ 1961

DOLLS

Graphic designer Marilyn Neuhart worked at the Eames Office for more than thirty years. In 1957, she began making dolls to relax after work. Two years later, in 1959, Alexander Girard commissioned her to create dolls for Herman Miller's Textiles & Objects shop. The colors—moss, pink, orange, and turquoise—embody Neuhart's playful approach to modernism, at the same time alluding to Mexican traditional crafts.

Sage Green

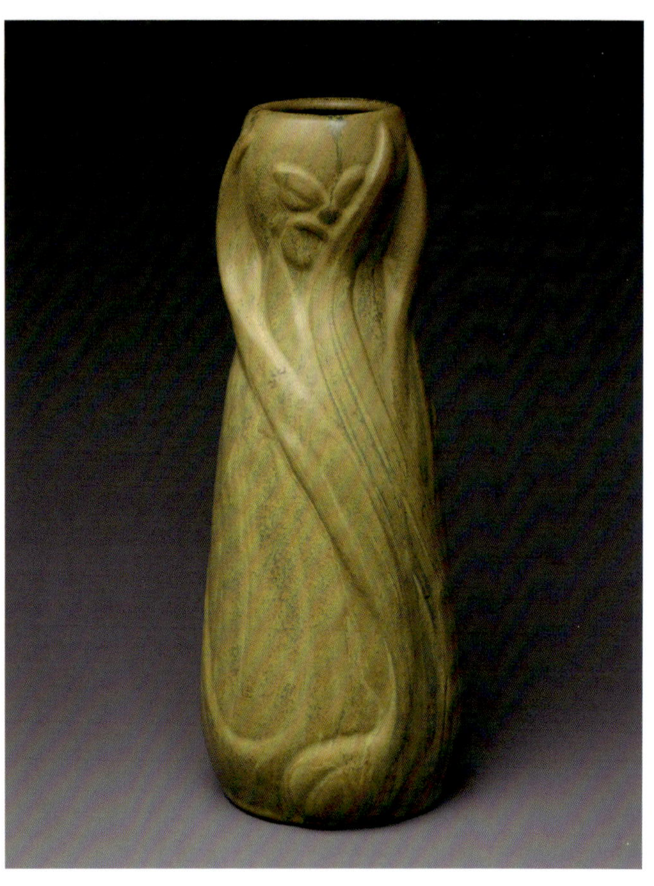

49

Vase with Daffodils

Artus van Briggle ~ 1902

VASE

After studying in Paris in the late 1890s, Artus van Briggle and his wife Anna moved to Colorado in 1901 and established a pottery studio in Colorado Springs. They gained recognition for their unique glazes, and their use of soft textures and unusual colors such as sage green. Van Briggle's early work reflected the Art Nouveau movement, especially in the sinuous curves of his floral vases.

EARTH COLORS

Tan

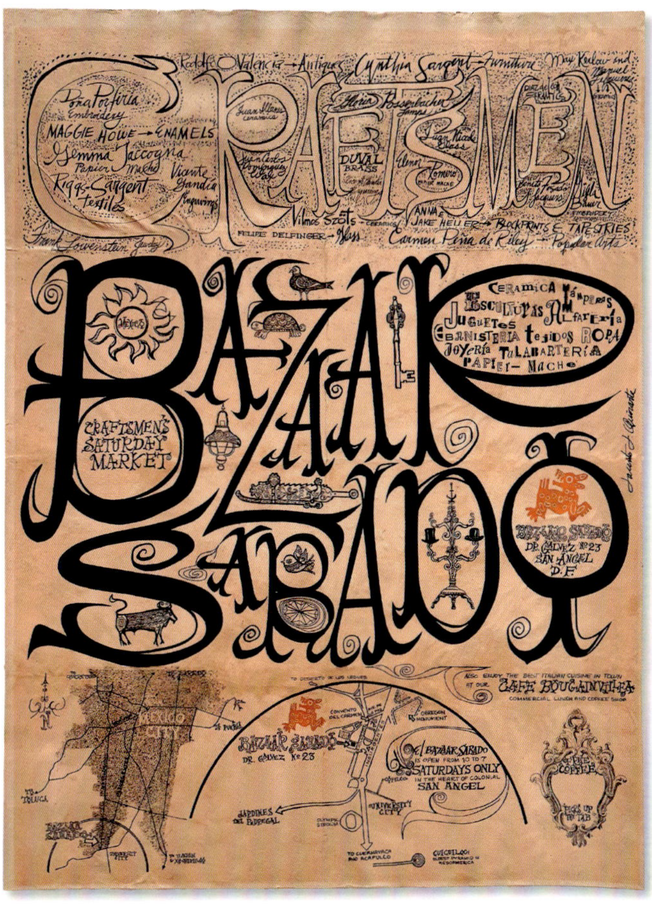

50

El Bazaar Sábado, San Ángel, Mexico City

Jacinto Quirarte ~ ca. 1965

POSTER

Jacinto Quirarte was a Mexican American art historian and professor who designed and illustrated materials for El Bazaar del Sábado. The space highlighted Mexican design, folk art, and contemporary crafts each Saturday. The low-fi, low-budget poster was designed with handmade typography, and printed with two colors on inexpensive tan paper. The design succeeds due to its raw vitality rather than glossy printing.

Coffee

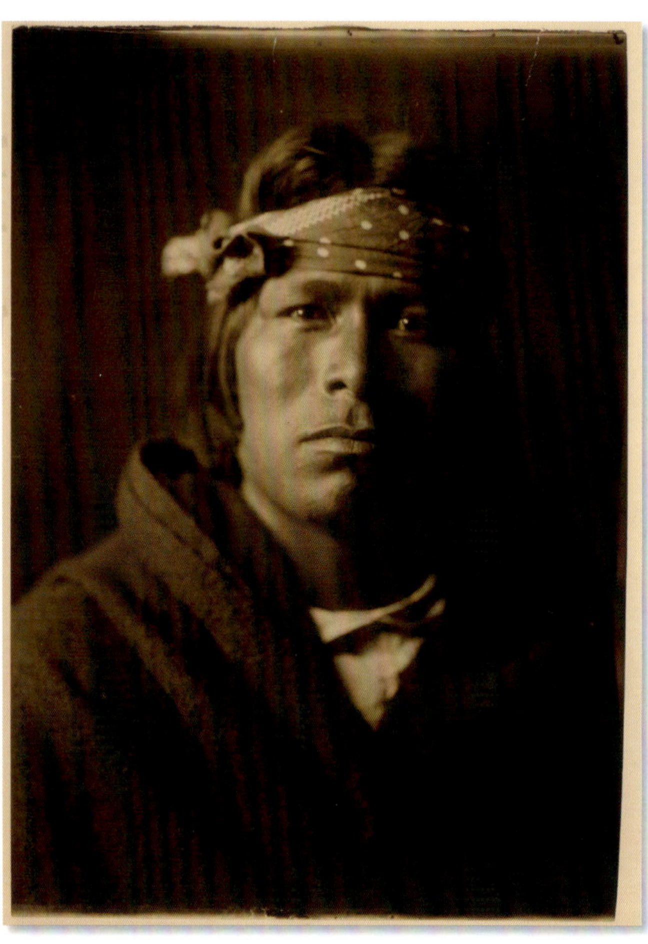

51

An Acoma Man

Edward S. Curtis ~ 1904

PHOTOGRAPH

For his work *The North American Indian,* Edward S. Curtis developed goldtone prints, or "Curt-Tones," which produced a distinct gold color. The project lasted forty years, encompassed forty volumes of images and text, and produced more than 40,000 photographs. Curtis applied a liquid emulsion to optical glass, projecting his negatives onto it, and used a mixture of banana oils and bronzing powders to achieve the effect.

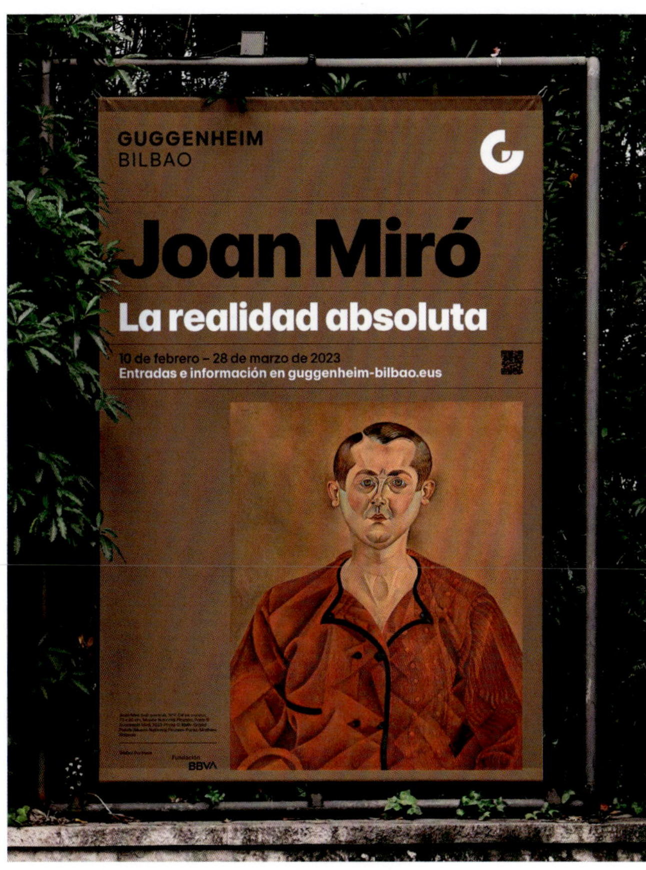

52

Guggenheim

Harry Pearce, Pentagram ~ 2023

IDENTITY SYSTEM

Pentagram's identity program for the Guggenheim is an abstract representation of the letter "G," inspired by the architectural design of the museums. Artist imagery is never cropped without consent, and typography is separated, avoiding any overlay on the art. Instead of using a strict color palette, color is employed strategically as an accent to the subject, such as the brown used in Joan Miró's *Self Portrait* from 1919.

EARTH COLORS

Burnt Umber

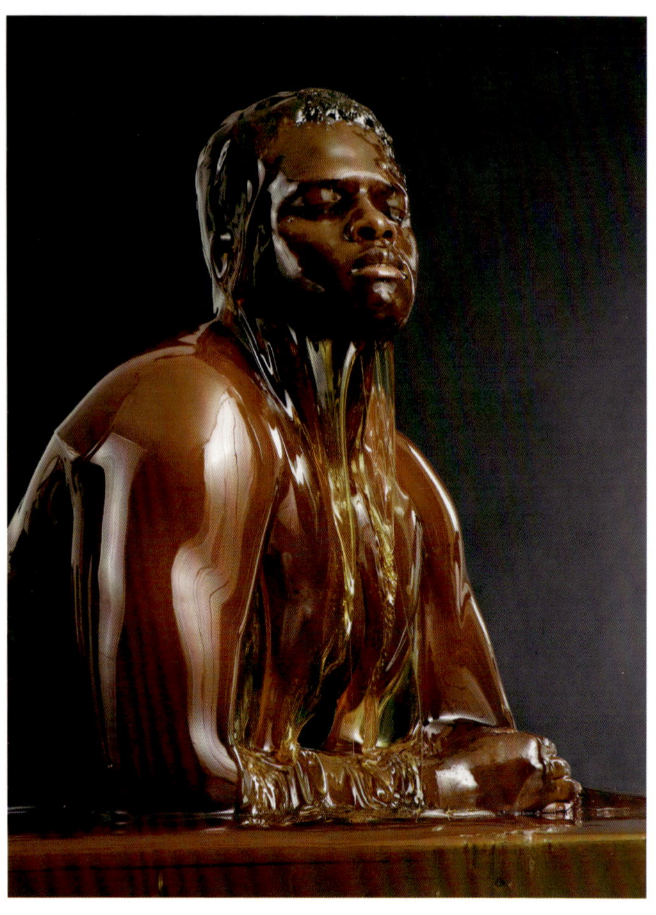

53

Isaiah, Upright

Blake Little ~ 2014

PHOTOGRAPH

Blake Little's photographic series, *Preservation*, examines themes of immortality, death, physical perfection, and repulsion. The subjects, coated in honey, have an appearance of objects preserved in amber, freezing them in time. The burnt umber and brown tones vary with the amount of honey and the subject's skin tone, making them unrecognizable, and transforming their unique features into something universal.

Chocolate

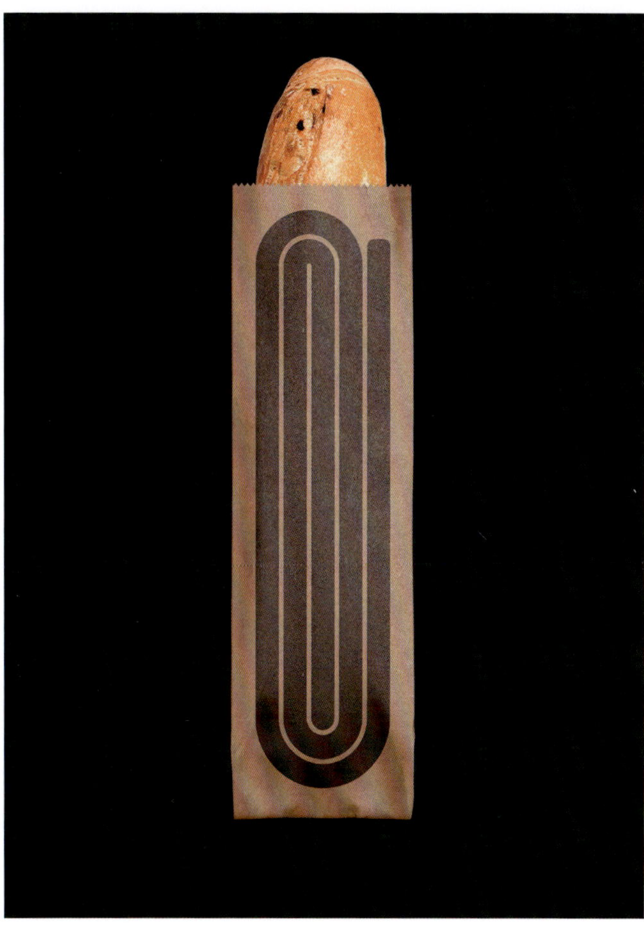

54

Antara 128

Mucho ~ 2023

PACKAGING

Antara 128 is an innovative bakery and restaurant located in central Melbourne, Australia. It combines European traditions with contemporary Australian influences. Mucho designed a dynamic symbol inspired by the process used in folding and rolling dough, which is essential for creating layered baked goods. The use of chocolate brown on brown kraft paper further emphasizes the theme of baking.

EARTH COLORS

Chestnut

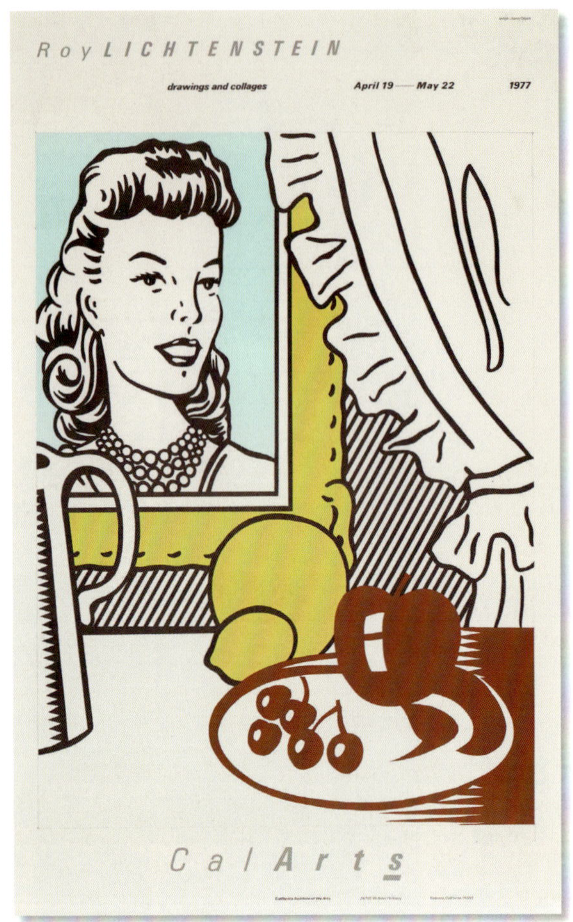

55

Roy Lichtenstein at CalArts

Jayme Odgers ~ 1977

POSTER

This poster features Roy Lichtenstein's *Still Life with Portrait (Study)* from 1973. During the Renaissance, artists often incorporated moral lessons into a still life. For artists like Lichtenstein the still life provided a commentary on consumerism and popular culture. Artist Jayme Odgers's minimal typography in light gray offsets the chestnut, yellow, and seafoam, while referencing the hard lines and angles of the image.

EARTH COLORS

Harvest Gold

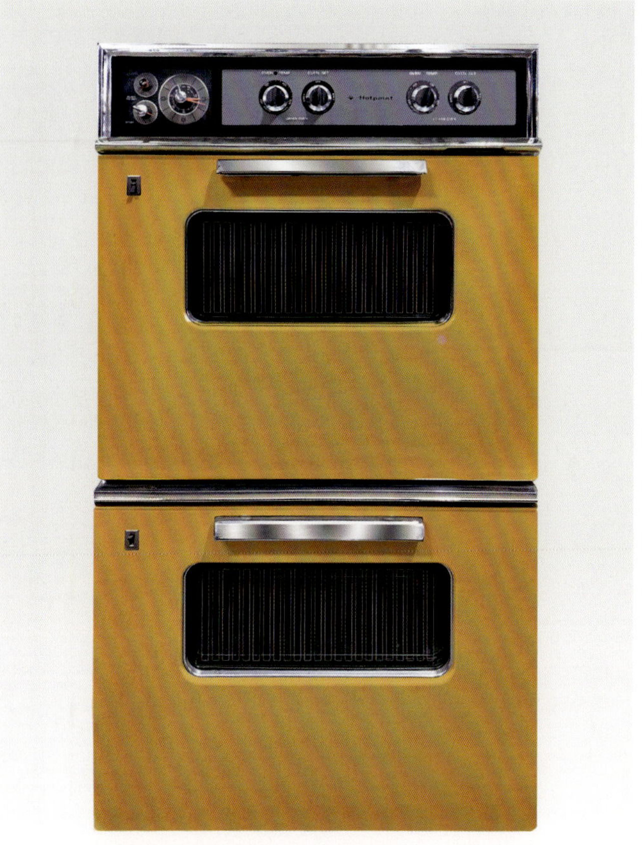

56

Hotpoint Double Wall Oven

Unknown ~ 1968

APPLIANCE

In 1968, Hotpoint introduced a new line of colors for ovens, refrigerators, dishwashers, and stoves: Avocado and Harvest Gold. Designed to appeal to fashion-oriented consumers, the colors became ubiquitous within years. Like the pastel tones of the 1950s, and psychedelic hues of the 1960s, Harvest Gold became one of the colors synonymous with the 1970s.

Ocher

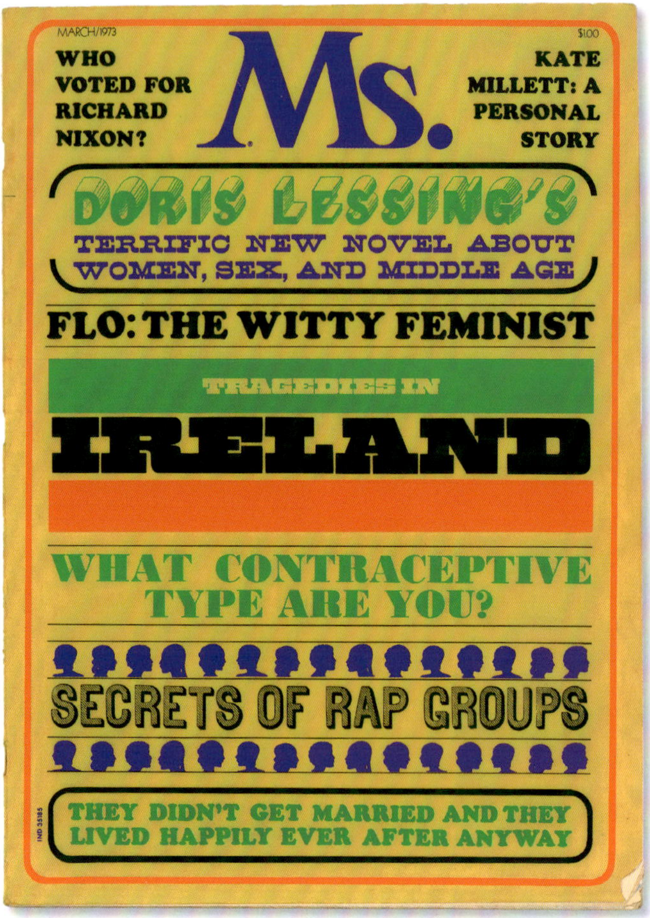

MARCH/1973 $1.00

Ms.

WHO VOTED FOR RICHARD NIXON?

KATE MILLETT: A PERSONAL STORY

DORIS LESSING'S TERRIFIC NEW NOVEL ABOUT WOMEN, SEX, AND MIDDLE AGE

FLO: THE WITTY FEMINIST

TRAGEDIES IN IRELAND

WHAT CONTRACEPTIVE TYPE ARE YOU?

SECRETS OF RAP GROUPS

THEY DIDN'T GET MARRIED AND THEY LIVED HAPPILY EVER AFTER ANYWAY

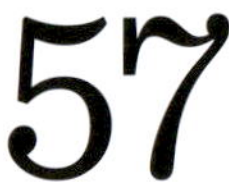

Ms. Magazine

Bea Feitler ~ 1973

MAGAZINE COVER

Ms. magazine was founded by activists Gloria Steinem and Dorothy Pitman Hughes in 1971, providing "feminist news and information." Bea Feitler's 1973 cover design departed from the standard fashion magazine formula of a young woman's face and headlines. She created a message-oriented, typographic symphony of multiple typefaces in complementary colors on an ocher background.

Wheat

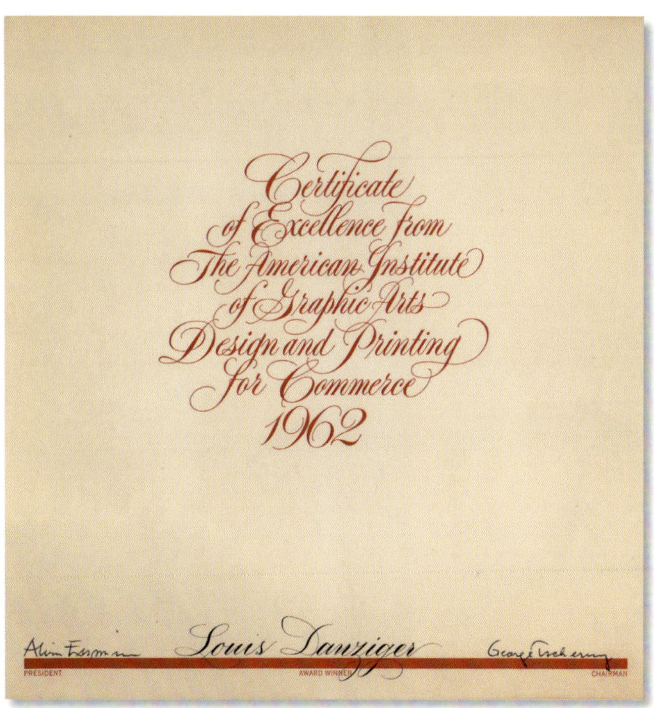

58

Certificate of Excellence, AIGA

Chairman, George Tscherny ~ 1962

AWARD

The American Institute of Graphic Arts (AIGA) is the oldest organization dedicated to communication arts in the world. Its mission was to promote excellence in graphic design through events, projects, and competitions. The award presented to graphic designer Louis Danziger showcases an early example of typographic eclecticism, featuring an elaborate script printed on wheat-colored stock.

NEUTRAL COLORS

Beige

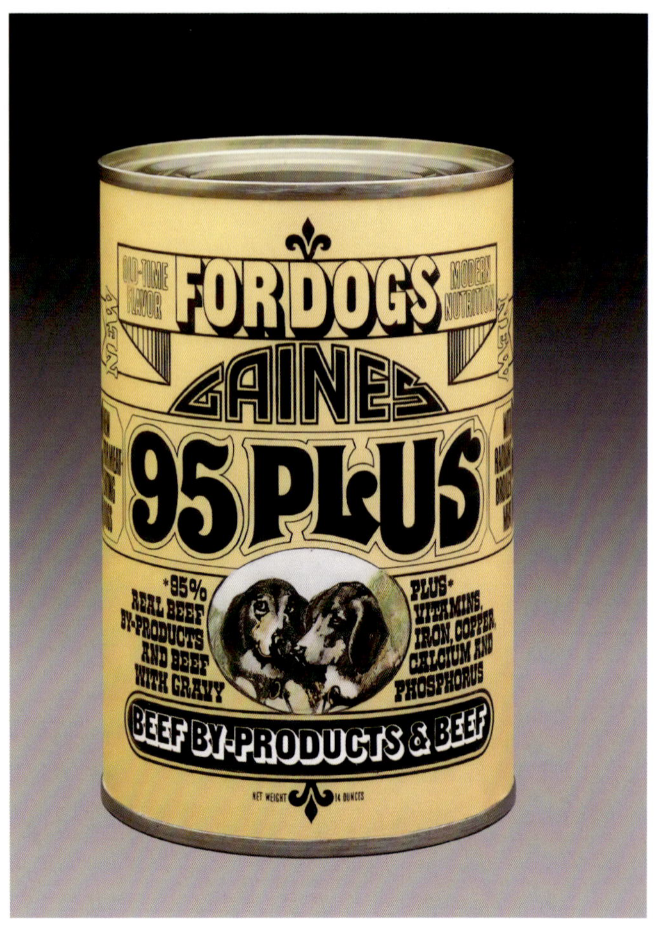

59

Gaines 95 Plus

Herb Lubalin ~ 1968

PACKAGING

Herb Lubalin designed this (rejected) prototype for a package of Gaines dog food. Lubalin used typography creatively to express ideas and evoke emotions rather than just simply to present information with no personality. Like the AIGA certificate (58 Wheat), Lubalin rejected a bright white background and modernist typography for this mix of typefaces on a beige background, evoking a sense of nostalgia.

NEUTRAL COLORS

Sandstone

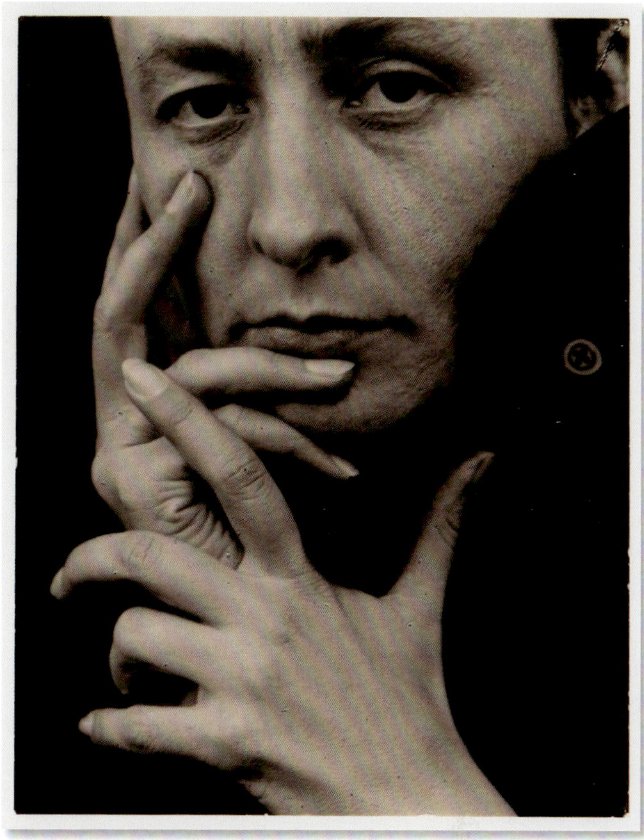

60

Georgia O'Keeffe

Alfred Stieglitz ~ 1918

PHOTOGRAPH

Alfred Stieglitz remarked that color in photography was as unnecessary as "lips on a woodpecker." However, he explored many printing methods and photographic papers to achieve a balance of colors: light gray to warm sandstone to pure black. As Stieglitz also said, "Every print I make, even from one negative, is a new experience, a new problem. For, unless I am able to vary—add—I am not interested."

Greige

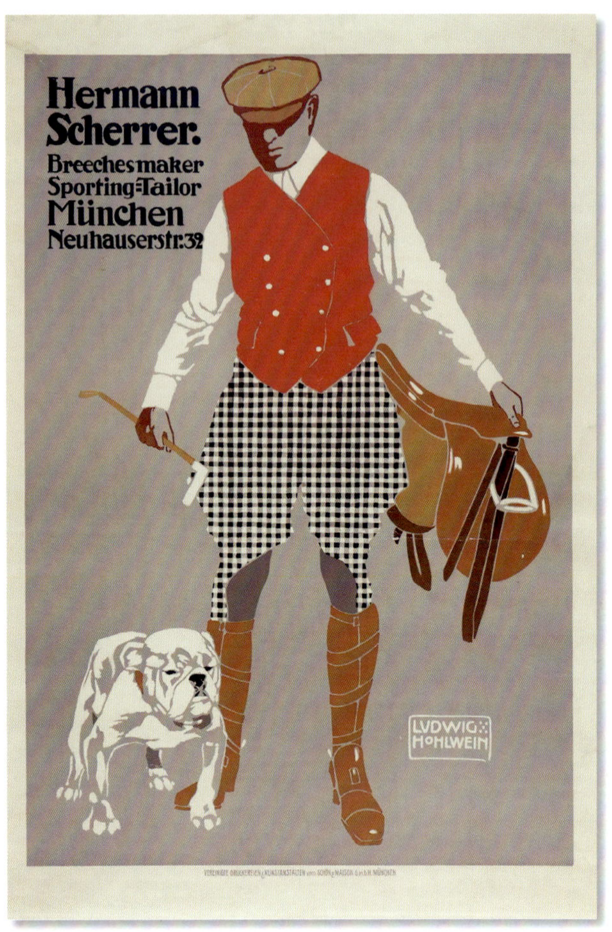

61

Hermann Scherrer

Ludwig Hohlwein ~ 1911

POSTER

At the beginning of the twentieth century, Ludwig Hohlwein introduced a minimal approach to poster and advertising design, *Plakatstil*, or poster style. Hohlwein designed this poster for a fashion company. It features implied space, large flat shapes and patterns, minimal details, and a reduced color palette of greige, red, chestnut, black, and white. The poster invites the viewer to fill in the missing visual information.

Putty

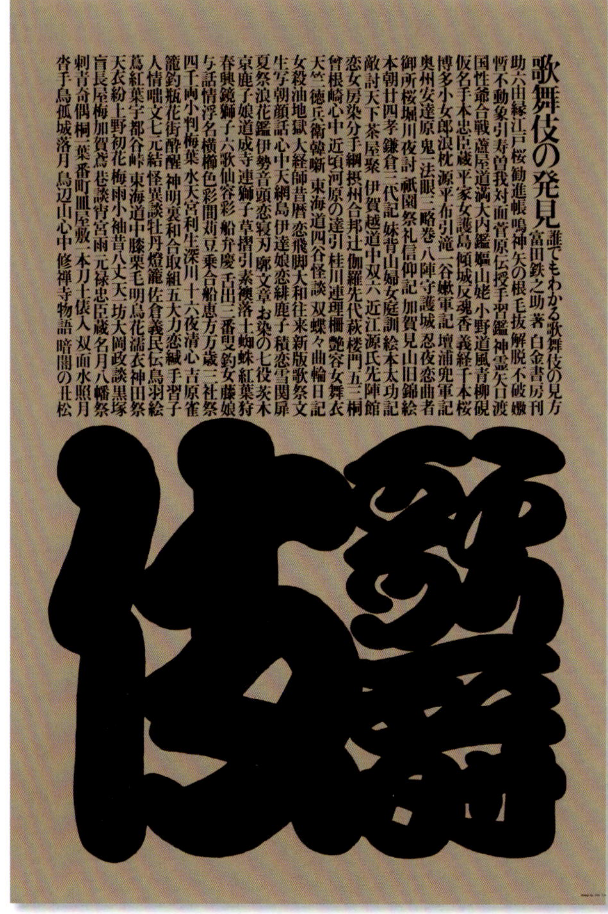

62

Page from the Kabuki Book

Ikko Tanaka ~ 1974

POSTER

This poster by Japanese designer Ikko Tanaka showcases traditional Japanese calligraphy, rendered in black *sumi-e* ink against a minimalist putty background. The intricate characters are artistically arranged to reflect the essence of Kabuki theater, seamlessly blending traditional and minimalist styles. Tanaka was a master of communicating a message with the fewest possible elements.

NEUTRAL COLORS

Pewter

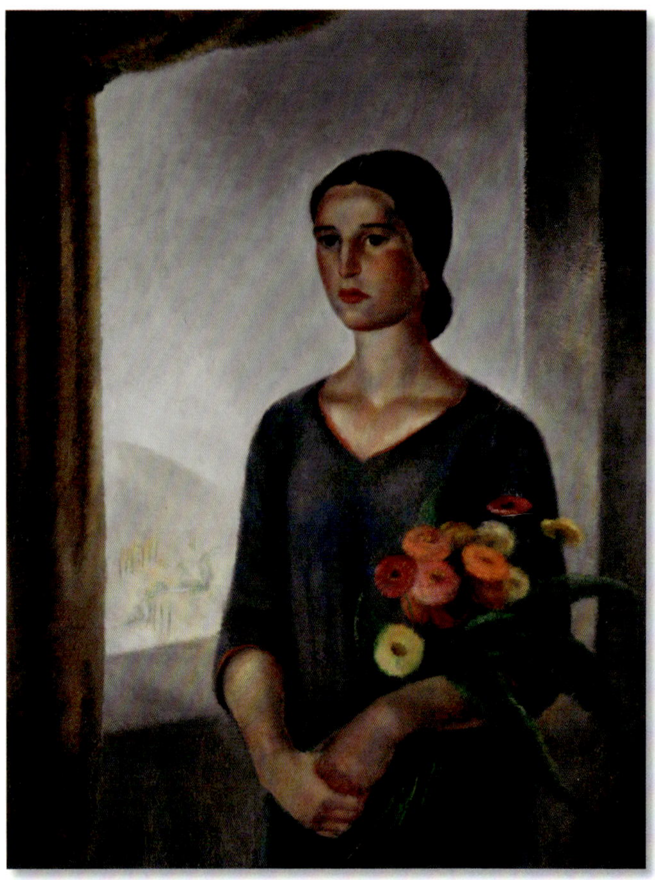

63

Francesca

Louise B. Maloney ~ 1927

PAINTING

Louise Maloney's painting technique brought an antique, muted, and gentle quality to her work. In her painting titled *Francesca,* Maloney draws inspiration from Leonardo da Vinci, while offering a contemporary perspective. The vibrant depiction of Francesca's face, neck, and the flowers she holds contrasts beautifully with the pewter-colored dress and background.

NEUTRAL COLORS

Slate

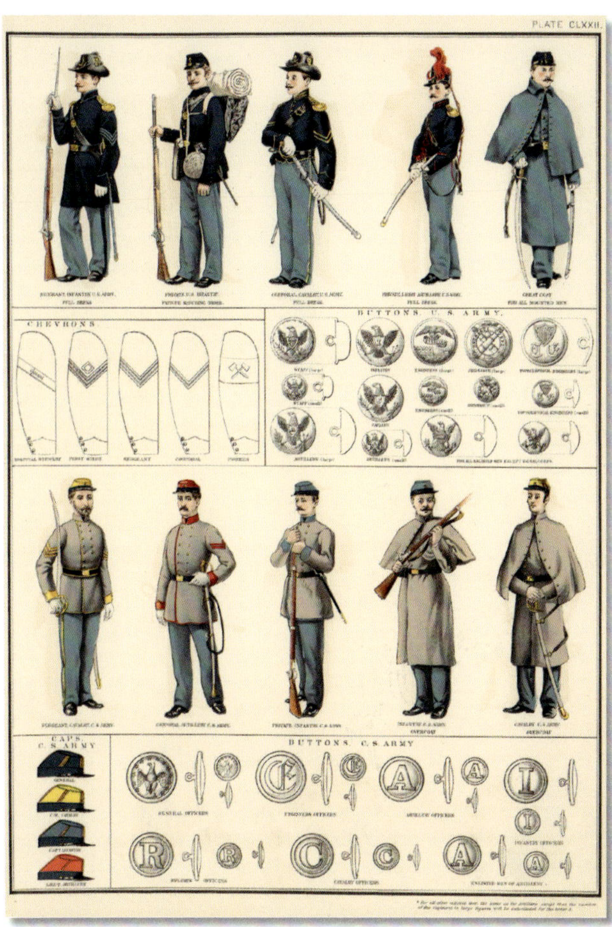

64

Plate 172

United States Department of War ~ 1895

LITHOGRAPH

Plate 172 of the *Atlas to Accompany the Official Records of the Union and Confederate Armies* features illustrations of the uniforms worn by soldiers during the American Civil War. The two sides are commonly identified by the colors of their official uniforms: Union soldiers typically wore blue and slate uniforms, while Confederate soldiers wore gray and blue.

NEUTRAL COLORS
Charcoal

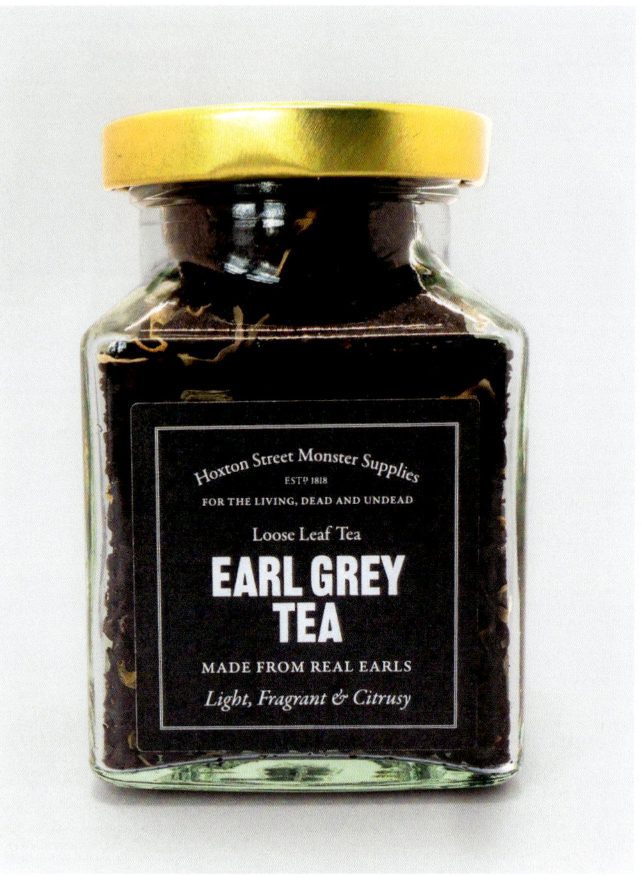

65

Hoxton Street Monster Supplies

We Made This ~ 2022

PACKAGING

Hoxton Street Monster Supplies is a charitable shop selling quality, kooky goods to monsters of every kind since 1818. All profits from Hoxton Street Monster Supplies are donated to the organization Ministry of Stories for their creative writing and mentoring work with children. We Made This designed packaging with classic colors such as charcoal and white, and elegant typography juxtaposing the conventional with the odd.

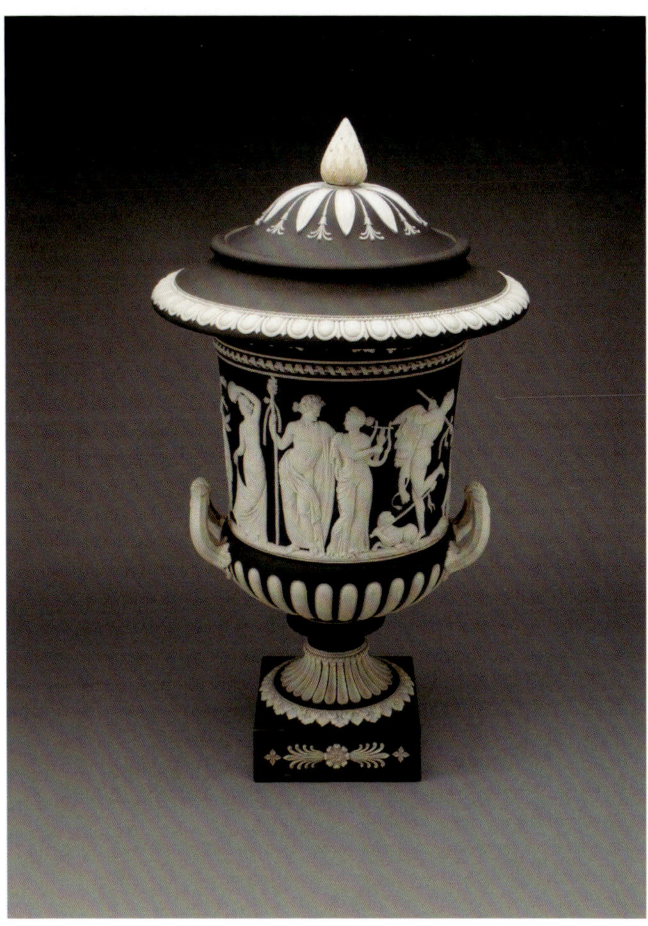

66

Wedgwood Borghese Vase

Josiah Wedgwood and Sons ~ 1850–1900

VASE

In 1774, Josiah Wedgwood developed Jasperware, which, unlike any other form of stoneware, could absorb colors throughout its body. Produced between 1850 and 1900, the vase is modeled on a marble version from ancient Greece. It has a white relief on a gray body that shows worshipers of Bacchus escorting the drunken minor deity Silenus. The vase was purchased by the Borghese family in 1566, and is named after them.

Light Gray

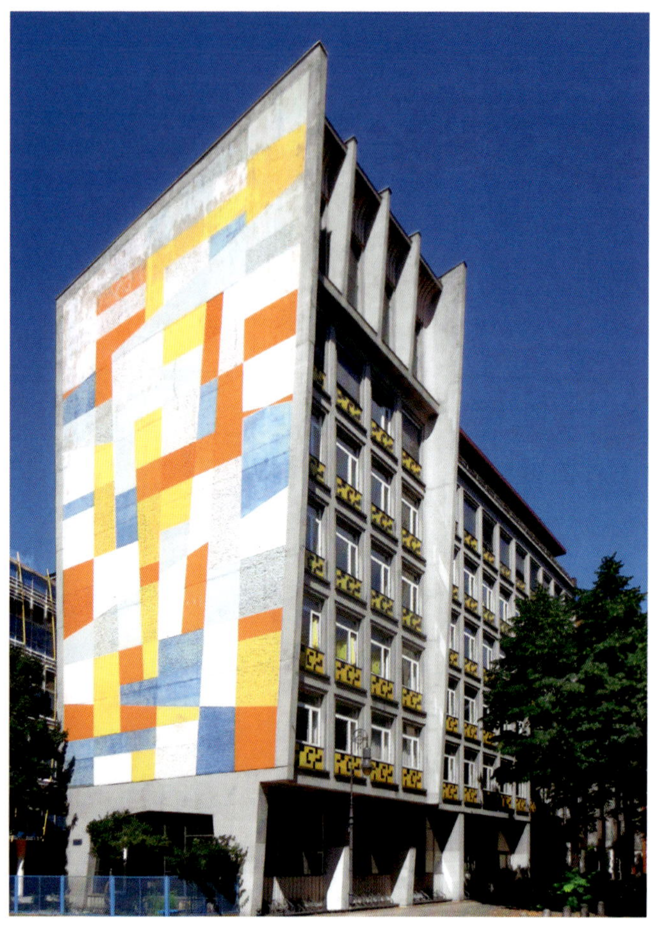

67

Katholische Schule Sankt Franziskus

Margot Zech-Weymann ~ 1959

ARCHITECTURE

Margot Zech-Weymann designed the Katholische Schule Sankt Franziskus with a striking feature: a windowless front wall facing Hohenstaufenstrasse in Berlin. The entire surface is a mural set against the light gray concrete of the structure. The building widens as it rises, giving it a dynamic appearance. Some pillars of the concrete structure also widen toward the top and extend prominently from the facade.

Parchment

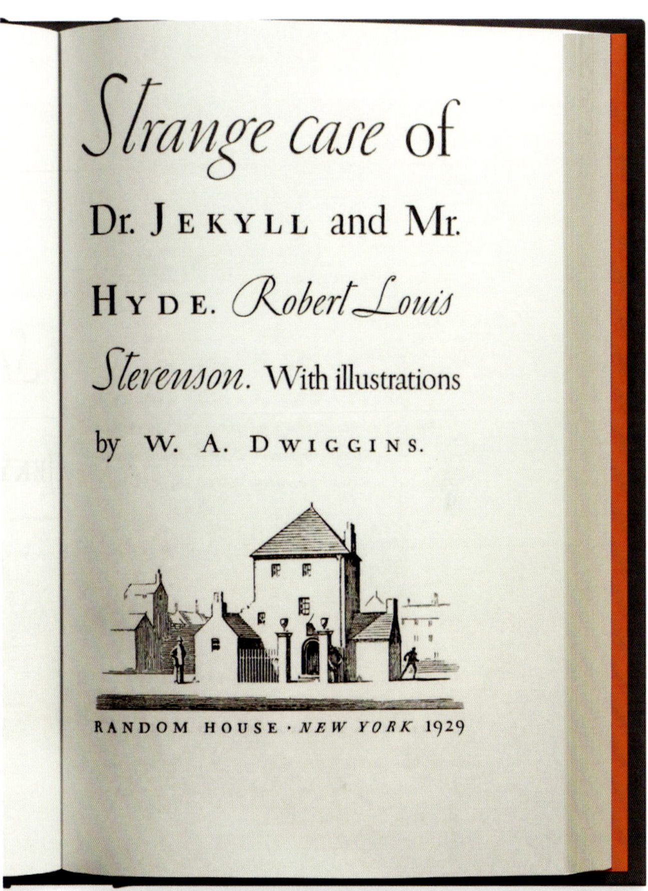

Strange case of
Dr. JEKYLL and Mr.
HYDE. Robert Louis
Stevenson. With illustrations
by W. A. DWIGGINS.

RANDOM HOUSE · NEW YORK 1929

68

Strange Case of Dr. Jekyll and Mr. Hyde

William Addison Dwiggins ~ 1929

BOOK

William Addison Dwiggins was an American type designer, calligrapher, and book designer renowned for his impeccable typography, such as that on the title page for *Strange Case of Dr. Jekyll and Mr. Hyde*. Dwiggins championed excellence in printing and book production at a time when books were increasingly mass produced. The paper here, a soft parchment color with a refined eggshell finish, demonstrates his commitment.

NEUTRAL COLORS

Sand

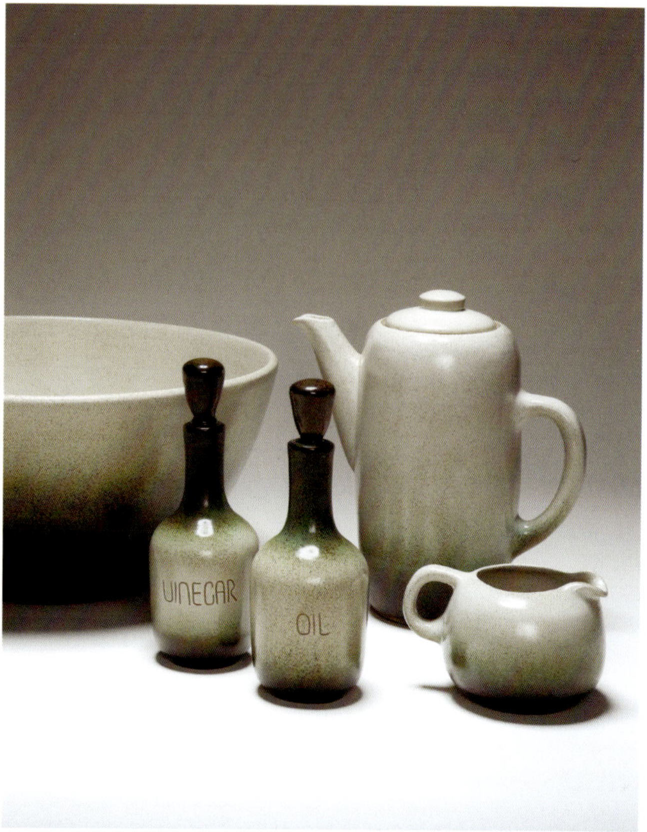

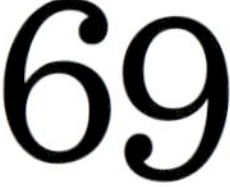

69

Selection of Accessories in Sea and Sand Glaze

Edith Heath, photography Jeffery Cross ~ 1950s

CERAMICS

Edith Heath founded Heath Ceramics in Sausalito, California, in 1948. She developed a glazing and firing technique that produced remarkably subtle shades in dinnerware. Like many postwar designers, Heath created functional and simple dinnerware, focusing on everyday items free from excessive decoration or unnecessary elements. Her straightforward approach included naming her pieces with such simple terms as "Sand."

NEUTRAL COLORS

Cream

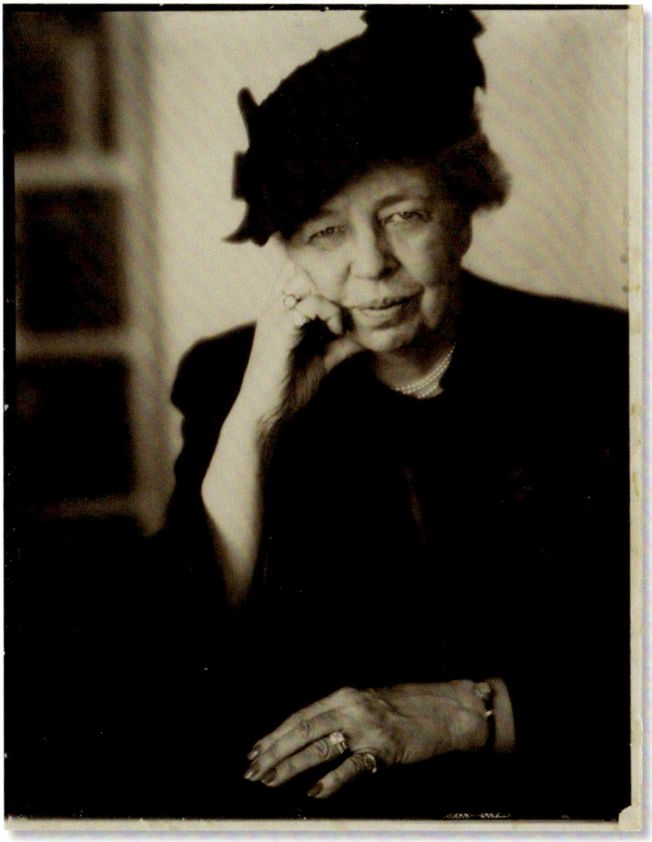

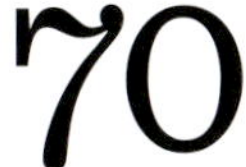

70

Eleanor Roosevelt

Clara Sipprell ~ 1949

PHOTOGRAPH

Through her career, Clara Sipprell remained committed to a pictorialist approach to photography with soft focus and an emphasis on beauty. She experimented with multiple printing methods, preferring the cream tones to a stark modernist white. Her photograph, *New York City, Old and New,* was the first work by a woman collected by the Museum of Modern Art. First Lady Eleanor Roosevelt admired and championed Sipprell.

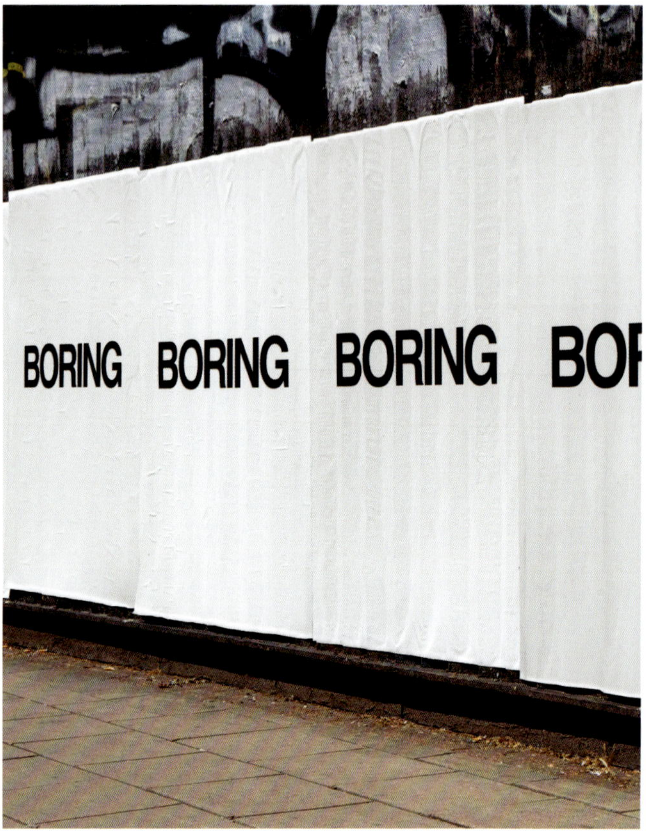

71

Boring

Unknown ~ 2023

CONSTRUCTION BARRICADE

These posters may reference John Baldessari's assignment given to students at Nova Scotia College of Art and Design in 1971: to write repeatedly on the gallery walls the phrase, "I will not make any more boring art." Alternatively, it may simply question the purpose of life or of walls and other boundaries.. Black Helvetica type on a white background may appear dull to some. However, minimalists will find it glorious.

Black

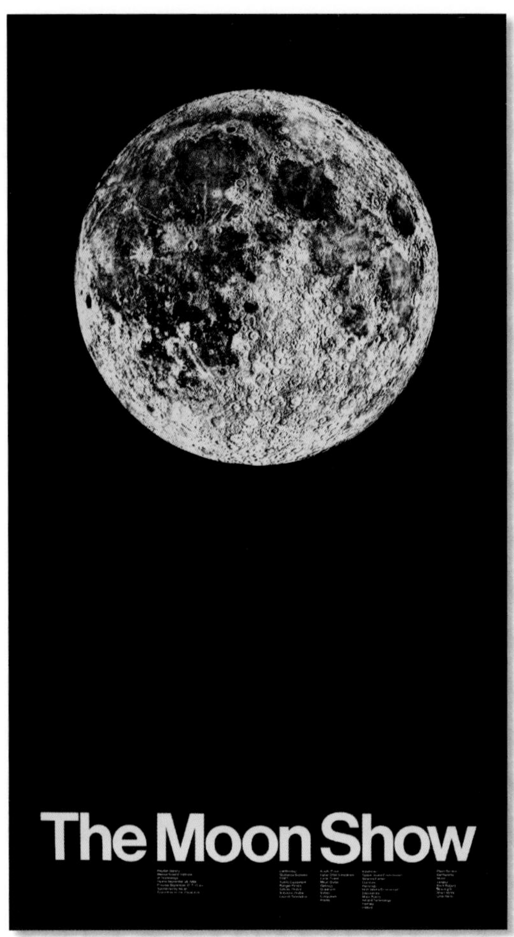

72

The Moon Show, MIT

Jacqueline Casey ~ 1969

POSTER

Jacqueline Casey was a prominent practitioner of the International Typographic Style during the 1960s and 1970s, influenced by Swiss designer Josef Müller-Brockmann, and led the Office of Publications at Massachusetts Institute of Technology. This poster for *The Moon Show* promoted a presentation on the Apollo 11 mission. The design displays her modernist sensibility with a black-and-white palette and single typeface.

SPECIAL COLORS

Fluorescent Pink

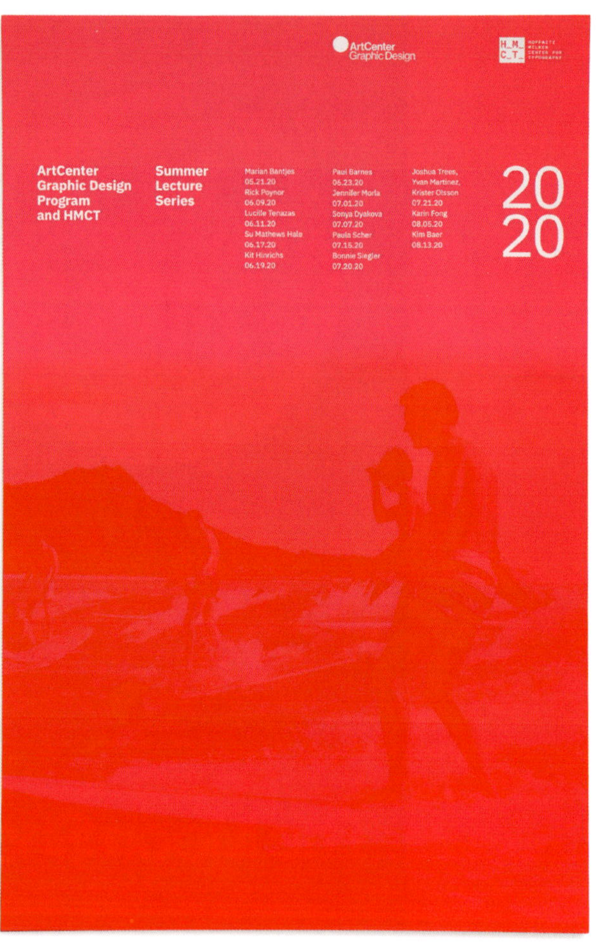

73

ArtCenter Summer Lecture Series

Sean Adams ~ 2020

POSTER

The Summer Lecture Series was organized by designers Jacqueline Casey and Josef Müller-Brockmann. Sean Adam's posters advertising the series embody a strict modernist approach. Their layout and typography follow a mathematically precise grid. The image of surfers reinforces the idea of summer. The modernist rigor is subverted with the intensity of fluorescent pink and red rather than the traditional tones of black, white, and red.

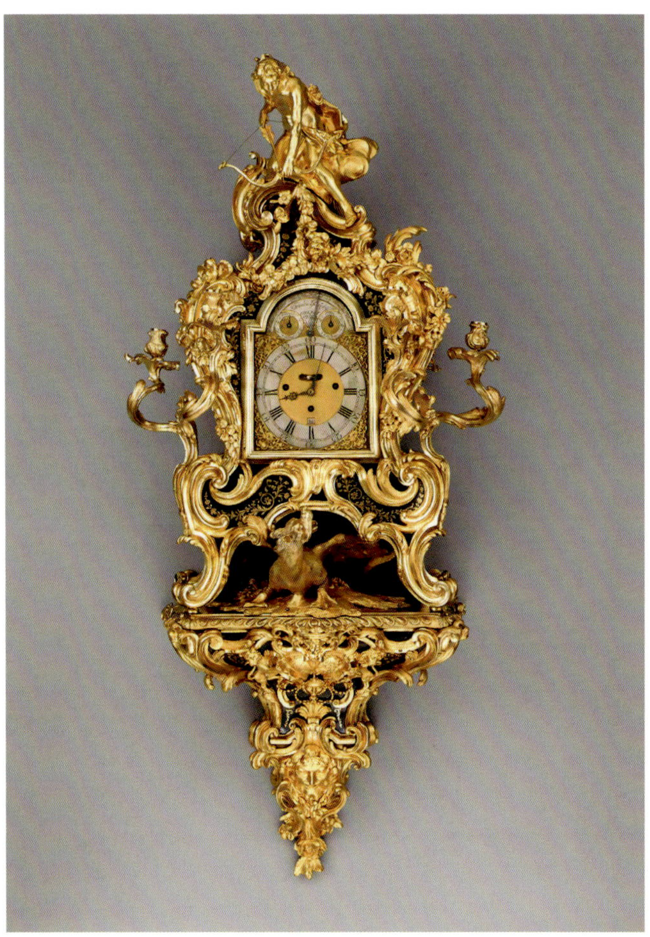

74

Wall Clock

Jean-Pierre Latz ~ ca. 1735–40

CLOCK

This gold, sculptural wall clock exemplifies the extravagance and luxury of the Louis XV era as an elaborate example of the French Rococo style. Expensive and ornate clocks such as this entertained the owner with a musical composition of six melody titles that are engraved in the dial's arch. The mythological scene shows the Greek god Apollo preparing to strike down the serpent Python.

SPECIAL COLORS

Silver

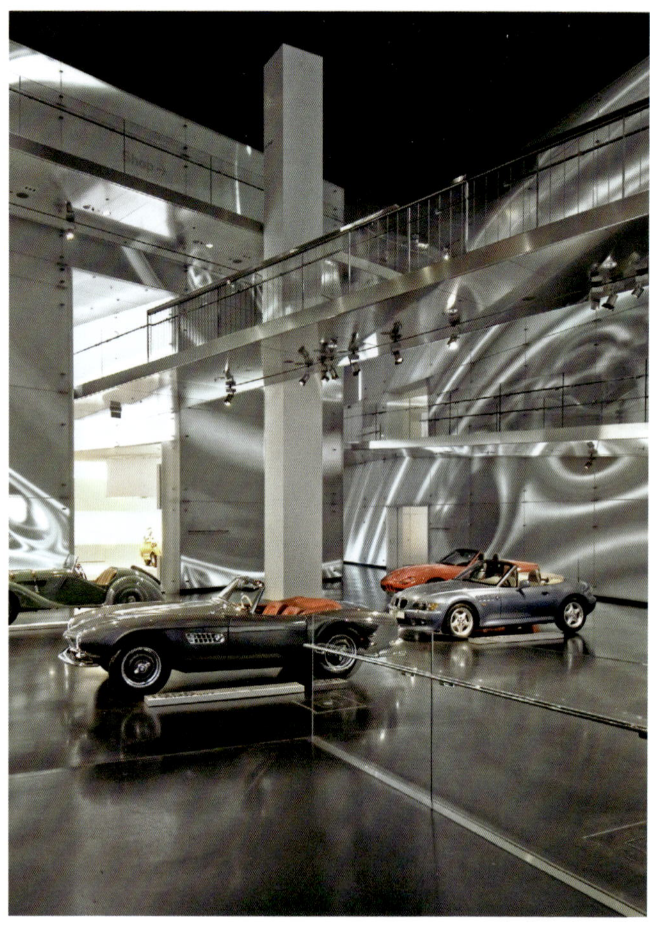

75

Spheres

ART+COM Studios ~ 2008

EXHIBITION

ART+COM Studios designed the exhibition, *Spheres*, at the BMW Museum in Munich. The space is framed by 7,500 square feet of wall space covered in white monochrome LEDs, concealed behind opaque glass, creating a dynamic facade. The design features 3D graphics and moving abstract images on the walls. The overall effect of a sparkling silver and white atmosphere serves as a backdrop for the historical vehicles.

Image Credits

Every effort has been made to trace copyright holders and to obtain their permission for the use of copyright material. The publisher apologizes for any errors or omissions in the below list and would be grateful if notified of any corrections that should be incorporated in future reprints or editions of this booklet and cards.

1. Courtesy Louis Danziger Design History Archives
2. © Collins
3. © Paula Scher, Pentagram
4. Courtesy Steven Treinen
5. Courtesy Sherman Adams
6. Collection of the author
7. Courtesy Letterform Archive
8. © Oscar Maia
9. Collection of the author
10. Photography by Šarūnas Burdulis
11. Courtesy Louis Danziger Design History Archives
12. Courtesy of Gail Anderson
13. Courtesy National Museum of American History
14. Courtesy Brooklyn Museum Costume Collection at The Metropolitan Museum of Art, Gift of the Brooklyn Museum, 2009; Gift of the estate of Mrs. Arthur F. Schermerhorn, 1957
15. © Collins
16. © Omni Design
17. Courtesy LaPrele Arlene Jeffs
18. Collection of the author
19. Collection of the author
20. © Amir Nikravan
21. Courtesy Herman Miller
22. Collection of the author
23. Photography by Matthias Bethke
24. Courtesy The J. Paul Getty Museum, Los Angeles
25. © Rebeca Méndez Studio
26. Courtesy The Metropolitan Museum of Art, Gift of Mr. and Mrs. Charles Wrightsman, 1970
27. © Debbie Millman
28. © Blok Design
29. Smithsonian Institution, Anacostia Community Museum, Photograph by Joseph Aaron Campbell
30. © Michael Boshnaick
31. Smithsonian Libraries and Archives
32. © Sean Adams
33. The Metropolitan Museum of Art, Friends of Asian Art Gifts, 2021
34. National Portrait Gallery, Smithsonian Institution
35. Collection of the Author
36. Courtesy Cleveland Museum of Art, Gift of the Norman W. Zaworski Trust
37. Courtesy Cleveland Museum of Art Bequest of Charles Maurer
38. © Brian White
39. © LucienneRoberts+ Lucienne Roberts and John McGill
40. Courtesy Louis Danziger Design History Archives
41. Courtesy Rago/Wright
42. © Roland Young
43. Collection of the author
44. The Metropolitan Museum of Art, The Walter H. and Leonore Annenberg Collection, Gift of Walter H. and Leonore Annenberg, 1993
45. Courtesy The Metropolitan Museum of Art, Edward C. Moore Jr. Gift, 1923
46. Photography by Sean Adams
47. Courtesy Art Institute of Chicago, Everett and Ann McNear Collection
48. Courtesy Rago/Wright
49. Courtesy The Metropolitan Museum of Art, Gift of Martin Eidelberg, 2020
50. Courtesy Louis Danziger Archives
51. Collection of the author
52. © Pentagram
53. © Blake Little
54. © Mucho-BPO
55. Collection of the author
56. Public domain
57. Courtesy Louis Danziger Design History Archives
58. Collection of the author
59. Courtesy Louis Danziger Design History Archives
60. Courtesy Art Institute of Chicago, Alfred Stieglitz Collection
61. Courtesy ArtCenter Library's Archives and Special Collections
62. Courtesy ArtCenter Library's Archives and Special Collections
63. Courtesy Cleveland Museum of Art, Hinman B. Hurlbut Collection, 1928

64. Collection of the author
65. © We Made This
66. Courtesy Art Institute of Chicago, Gift of James Viles
67. Photography by Sean Adams
68. Courtesy Louis Danziger Design History Archives
69. © Heath Ceramics, photography, Jeffery Cross
70. National Portrait Gallery, Smithsonian Institution; bequest of Phyllis Fenner
71. Photography by Sean Adams
72. Courtesy Louis Danziger Design History Archives
73. © Sean Adams
74. Courtesy Art Institute of Chicago, Ada Turnbull Hertle Fund
75. © Art+Com

For Abrams
Editor: Juliet Dore
Design Manager: Jenice Kim
Managing Editor: Amy Vinchesi
Production Manager: Larry Pekarek

For Quarto
Publisher: James Evans
Editorial Director: Isheeta Mustafi
Managing Editor: Lucy Tipton
Editor: Nick Pierce
Art Director: Emily Nazer
Publishing Operations Director: Kathy Turtle
Production Controller: George Li

Library of Congress Control Number: 2025934440
ISBN: 978-1-4197-8485-9
eISBN: 979-8-88707-896-0

The principal typeface used on the cards and booklet is Sentinel, designed by Jonathan Hoefler and Tobias Frere-Jones in 2009. Sentinel is based on earlier Egyptian or Slab Serif typefaces such as Clarendon designed by Robert Besley in 1845.

The color swatches contained in the book are as accurate as possible. However, due to the nature of the four-color printing process, on-screen-based RGB differences, and specific PANTONE® Colors, slight variations can occur.

Printed and bound in Shenzhen, Guangdong, China
DC/Nov/2025
10 9 8 7 6 5 4 3 2 1

ABRAMS is represented in the UK and Europe by Abrams & Chronicle Books, 1 West Smithfield, London EC1A 9JU and Média-Participations, 57 rue Gaston Tessier, 75166 Paris, France.

www.abramsandchronicle.co.uk and
www.media-participations.com
info@abramsandchronicle.co.uk

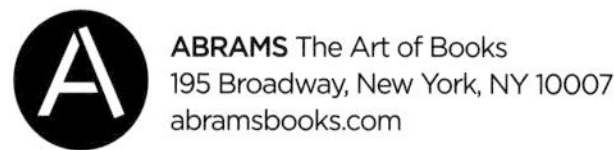